FOOD LOVERS' SERIES

Food Lovers' Guide to Atlanta

First Edition

The Best Restaurants, Markets &
Local Culinary Offerings

Malika Harricharan

gpp

Guilford, Connecticut

Editor: Amy Lyons
Project Editor: Meredith Dias
Layout Artist: Mary Ballachino
Text Design: Sheryl Kober
Illustrations © Jill Butler with additional art by Carleen Moira Powell
Maps: Trailhead Graphics, Inc. © Morris Book Publishing, LLC

ISBN 978-0-7627-7311-4

Printed in the United States of America
10 9 8 7 6 5 4 3 2 1

All the information in this guidebook is subject to change. We recommend that you call ahead to obtain current information before traveling.

Contents

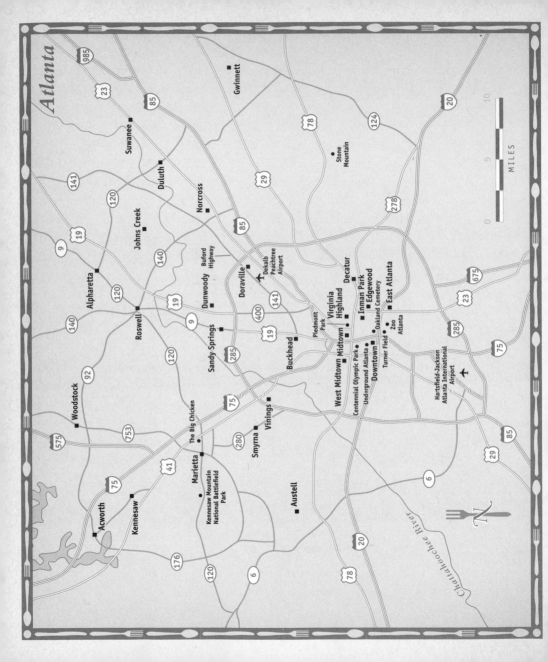

About the Author

Malika Harricharan has covered the Atlanta food scene at *Atlanta Restaurant Blog* (http://atlanta-restaurantblog.com) for nearly four years and has been an Atlanta resident since 1985. Malika has also written for Patch.com (a division of AOL) as well as *West Cobb Magazine*. In addition to keeping Atlantans up to date on the all things food-related, Malika is also the Founder and Managing Editor of the Association of Food Bloggers (http://associationof foodbloggers.org), a directory and online community serving food bloggers across the globe, helping them to become better writers, bloggers, and social media wizards.

Malika believes that an exceptional meal can be found just as easily at a hole in the wall as in swanky establishments. When she's not traveling the world and seeking out hidden foodie gems (or eating her way through Atlanta), she works as a social media consultant, creating, writing, and managing blogs, websites, Facebook/ Twitter pages, videos, and e-newsletters for various clients. She lives in Atlanta.

Acknowledgments

To Glen: Thank you for allowing me to drag you all around the city, not only for the purpose of this book, but in the years prior to my writing this book, while I blogged tirelessly about our experiences. Thank you for being my photographer, my plus-one at media events, my rock when I've wanted to give up, and for never complaining through it all.

To my Dad, John: Thank you for encouraging me my entire life to write and pursue the interests I feel passionate about. Thanks for sharing your wisdom with me and always being there to guide me. I feel truly blessed and fortunate to be your daughter.

To my brother, Jonathan, and Aunt Anita: Thanks for all your support throughout the years. It has meant so much to me.

To all of my friends, especially Steve: Thanks for waiting patiently for me to take all my pictures before digging in and allowing me to drag you to those out-of-the-way eateries. Most of all, thanks for spurring me on to follow my dream.

To Mike Ward and Keren Brown: Thanks for your words of kindness and encouragement from miles away. They meant more than you'll ever know.

To the Atlanta food community (chefs, servers, restaurateurs, my fellow food bloggers, and food critics): I hope you can glean just how much I love Atlanta and our diverse and thriving food scene from the words written here.

Introduction

There are over 30 streets in Atlanta named Peachtree. To some we are known as the Peach State, although Georgia isn't number one in peach pro- duction. If you've never been to Atlanta, you may think it is full of Southern food, like shrimp 'n' grits and fried okra. While these Southern favorites can be found, Atlanta has so much more to offer. Atlanta serves quite an eclectic mix of foods thanks to our diverse population, talented chefs, and foodie community.

Atlanta is the hub of the southeastern United States, with the world's busiest airport, the second-largest convention center in the world, and the home offices of many large corporations like Delta, Home Depot, and Coca-Cola, just to name a few. And with the large number of visitors to Atlanta, it is paramount that there is a diverse cuisine available for these discerning tourists. However, the popula- tion of 5 million, which includes the metro area, demands a variety of upscale dishes, too.

Atlanta boasts many award-winning chefs, including some that have been featured on TV shows like *Top Chef* and a myriad of Food Network shows. Most have chosen to remain in Atlanta and continue to share their skills with us, whether taking the helm at a well-known, established restaurant or starting their own unique concept. Atlanta foodies and bloggers are extremely supportive of these talented folks and spread the word about new ventures to keep others in the know.

Social media continue to play an important role in the spread of foodie news. New food bloggers come on the scene regularly, and there are quite a few foodie Tweeters as well. Their opinions matter to their loyal followers even more than those of restaurant critics. Blogger meetups and Tweetups are a common occurrence and can quickly transform an unknown restaurant into a hot spot.

We Atlantans love our burgers, pizza, and barbecue. These are casual comfort foods that can be enjoyed by all and bring groups together. Even though we are surrounded by these types of restaurants, we always welcome newcomers, whether they are traditional or have a unique spin on a tried-and-true concept like the Korean BBQ burger at Richard Blais's Flip Burger Boutique. However, we still appreciate the finer foods; many of us don't blink an eye at the thought of eating veal sweetbreads or bone marrow.

When I moved to Atlanta in 1985, I remember stopping on the roadside to buy peaches and tomatoes from homeowners who grew them as a hobby. That all vanished as people began purchasing their fruits and vegetables (whether seasonal or not) from large grocers. But in recent years, Atlantans have realized the importance of eating fresh foods that haven't been treated with harmful pesticides or growth hormones. This has led to not only backyard gardens in homes but also chefs who embrace the trend, buying fresh, organic produce from local markets or even adding gardens to their restaurants to grow their own herbs. It has been a pleasure to see the food cycle come full circle.

Atlanta also experienced its very first Food & Wine Festival in May 2011. Chefs came from as far west as Texas and as far north as Virginia to participate. The festival solidified to the rest of the country that Atlanta is truly a culinary destination and so much more than fried foods and moonshine. A big part of the festival involved food trucks, which have exploded in Atlanta.

The love of food has turned a passion into a livelihood for some Atlanta residents, even pushing them into a new profession that they may not have intended. Not many would disagree that our economy changed forever after 2007. Even extremely educated and experienced people were forced out of their jobs, which spawned careers some never knew were in them and helped shape the food scene of Atlanta. Some of these include food trucks, catering and secret suppers, and underground food events that would not exist had it not been for those fearless individuals who took on a new career.

So, who is this book for? Really anyone who has an interest in food and wants to further explore what Atlanta has to offer. Whether you are in Atlanta for a couple days, a new transplant unsure of where to start your food exploration, or someone who's lived in the city for a while, this book can serve as a guide. If you've only got a couple days in Atlanta but want to make sure you explore destinations off the beaten path, this guidebook will help. And if you've lived in Atlanta for years and have always wanted to explore the ethnic mecca that is Buford Highway, there are lots of restaurants listed that can serve as a guide for you, too. My hope is that you will explore places outside your comfort zone, whether that is taking a cab to an unfamiliar neighborhood in search of a fabulous dining experience or the taste of a new cuisine you haven't yet had the courage to try.

How to Use This Book

This guide is organized by neighborhoods or districts within the Atlanta metro area (see the Overview map on p. iv):

Buckhead
Downtown
Virginia Highland/Inman Park
Midtown
Gwinnett/Decatur
Buford Highway
Cobb & Northwest Atlanta
    (Marietta, Smyrna, Vinings,
    Woodstock, Kennesaw,
    Acworth)
Sandy Springs, Roswell & Alpharetta

> ### HELPFUL TIP
>
> In the back of the book there is an appendix organizing establishments by cuisine (see p. 233).

Price Code

$	Cheap eats: quick bites and entrees under $10 (even at dinner)
$$	A pretty good deal: entrees $10 to $16
$$$	Getting up there: entrees $16 to $28
$$$$	Splurgeville: entrees above $28 or prix-fixe menus at $40 or higher

Note: At lunchtime, $$ and $$$ places usually become $ and $$ places, respectively, with only slightly smaller portion sizes.

Within the chapters you'll find these categories:

Foodie Faves

These are restaurants where you'd go for tasty, interesting food, without breaking the bank, a few times per week. Foodie Faves can be bistros, Indian buffets, haute burger joints, tapas bars, Italian trattorias, even your neighborhood sandwich shop, if it's doing something outstanding.

Landmarks

Look here for the classics—barbecue joints, old-school steak houses, and other historic pillars of the Atlanta culinary landscape.

Specialty Stores & Markets

This is our "et cetera" category, not only for things like farmers' markets and wine shops, but also for the one-trick ponies of the food service business (e.g., bread bakeries).

Looking For A Deal?
Check Out Scoutmob

Scoutmob is a mobile app that acts as a portal to deals all over the city. The deals can range from restaurants to goods and services but the majority are for restaurants. Scoutmob highlights cool things to do in each city, so it helps locals discover stores and restaurants that they would not have known about otherwise. The real cool thing is the 50 percent–off deals available each day that cost the user nothing. Simply sign up on their site, and you'll be notified of the daily deals through their mobile app, via e-mail, or cell (they won't spam you).

"The deals are our business, but the content is strictly stuff we find interesting, curious, weird, funny, awesomely awesome, or just straight up informative."—Scoutmob site

What makes Scoutmob different from other discount programs? The cost: zilch. Other sites require users to buy a coupon or certificate, which gives them a discount when they spend a certain dollar amount. Scoutmob is absolutely free. There are virtually no restrictions for its use. Deals can be used anytime for anything from drinks to appetizers.

Keeping Up with Atlanta Food News

Amy on Food (http://amyonfood.blogspot.com). Amy Fox is an attorney by day, and food blogger by night. She shares her restaurant experiences as well as her own culinary endeavors with her readers.

You don't even need to print them out if using your phone. Keep in the mind the deals are only good for 3 months (on average), but since users pay nothing for them, it really doesn't matter if they expire without ever being used, as new deals are continuously being added.

Got an iPhone? Scoutmob has an app (available on iPhones and Droids) that will send all the deals directly to your phone without having to sign up each day. Just pull it up and show to your server or cashier; no need to print it out, either.

Without the mobile app, you'll need to go to the Scoutmob website and claim the deal and have it e-mailed or texted to you. However, it is still not much effort to get 50 percent off a meal.

Whether you are living in Atlanta or just visiting, it is well worth downloading the app or signing up for their daily e-mail list. While some of the daily deals are for places that are relatively unknown, some are well-known, popular destinations, and the cost savings can be quite substantial.

Atlanta Restaurant Blog (http://atlanta-restaurantblog.com). My food blog has been the source for restaurant reviews and foodie news since 2008. It features the occasional restaurant recipe, and there is a weekly restaurant review along with listings of food happenings and events in Atlanta and the surrounding area.

Blissful Glutton (www.blissfulglutton.com). Jennifer Zyman has been blogging since 2005 and also is a food critic for *Creative Loafing,* a free print newspaper that serves as a guide to Atlanta music, with movie reviews and restaurant reviews, among other things.

Chow Down Atlanta (www.chowdownatlanta.com). One of the longest running blogs in Atlanta, author Chloe Morris focuses on ethnic cuisines in the area. Special highlights are Korean, Chinese, Japanese, and Vietnamese cuisines.

Eat Buford Highway (http://eatbufordhighway .com). As the name suggests, this blog details the various restaurants and specialty stores in Atlanta's ethnic mecca, Buford Highway.

Eat It, Atlanta (www.eatitatlanta.com). Written by talented at-home cook Jimmy Sobeck, the site is very well written and highlights some unique finds as well as cooking techniques.

Food Near Snellville (www.foodnearsnellville.com). A very comprehensive dining list with reviews of restaurants in Atlanta. The site focuses on more obscure restaurants rather than the much-hyped ones.

365 Atlanta (www.365atlanta.com). The site was started by a local realtor in an effort to highlight different things to do in the city (there's something new each day) for those who are newly relocated here.

What Now, Atlanta (www.whatnowatlanta.com). Another site on the dining scene, this is written by founder Caleb Spivak. The site focuses on what there is to see and do in Atlanta. It also makes mention of health inspections and the latest openings and closings of Atlanta area restaurants.

TWITTER

@365Atlanta	@BlissfulGlutton
@ATL_Events	@SavoryExposure
@ATLEatsNTweets	@WhatNowAtlanta

Events

Atlanta is a very active city that is blessed with warm weather from early spring to late fall, which allows for many outdoor festivals. Many of these festivals center around food. They are listed below according to when they occur.

For a current list of events in Atlanta, contact the **Atlanta Convention and Visitors Bureau** at www.atlanta.net.

February

Oysterfest Atlanta (www.steamhouselounge.com/ oysterfest.html). An all-day event that takes place in Atlanta, although the venue has changed from year to year. Besides sampling different types of oysters, attendees can sample beer and hear live music. Tickets should be purchased in advance and are not inclusive of food or drinks. Geared to adults; kiddies should be left at home.

March

Baconfest (www.dadsgarage.com). This pork-lover event takes place in late March in the parking lot of Dad's Garage Theater, an improvisational comedy theater. Entertainment includes live music, improv games, and eating contests. Various price levels start at $25 for a taste sampling and increase to all you can eat and drink. The festival takes place rain or shine. No kids or dogs allowed. This event sells out each year, so purchasing tickets in advance is strongly recommended.

Tour of Kitchens (www.jlatlanta.org/?nd=2011_tok). Taking place over 2 days in mid-March, this self-guided tour is sponsored by the Junior League of Atlanta and promises appearances and demonstrations by legendary Atlanta chefs. The tour highlights some of the more modern features of high-end homes scattered throughout Atlanta and is perfect for anyone looking for inspiration for their own kitchen remodel. Tickets should be purchased ahead of time.

April

Dogwood Festival (www.dogwood.org). The first of many spring festivals in Atlanta, the Dogwood Festival is one of the most anticipated. Many look forward to its many activities that appeal to a wide audience. The festival features artwork from more than 200 artists, live music, and an activity zone for kids. Foodies will enjoy samples from plenty of local restaurants. Some homeowners also open up their beautiful homes as part of the festival. Fun for the entire family.

Inman Park Festival (www.inmanparkfestival.org). The Inman Park Festival and Tour of Homes takes place the last weekend in April. At Inman Park (Euclid Avenue at Elizabeth Street in Atlanta), the festival not only has lots of arts and crafts, a street market, and live entertainment, but even a parade. The parade is scheduled for Saturday afternoon around 2 p.m. and is headed up by the festively dressed Inman Park Butterfly. There'll be lots of good food on hand and even a tour of historic Atlanta homes. These are some of Atlanta's oldest homes that have been kept up very nicely or restored to pristine condition. Note that while the festival itself is free, the home tour requires a ticket purchase of around $15.

Sweetwater 420 Festival (www.sweetwater420fest.com). This 3-day festival celebrating Earth Day takes place at Candler Park, 1500 McLendon Ave. Northeast, in Atlanta. Besides beer, food, and live music, there is an artist's market that includes clothes, jewelry, accessories, and other goodies. Admission is free, but festivalgoers who want to sample beer must purchase a $5 wristband.

May

Atlanta Food & Wine Festival (www.atlfoodandwinefestival
.com). Inspired by the Food & Wine Classic in Aspen, this is the
most exciting festival in Atlanta as far as foodies are concerned.
Drawing festivalgoers from not only different states but different
countries, it is a celebration of the new South and the popularity of
its food and talent of its chefs. Guests get to sip, taste, and learn
about Southern food through a series of well-planned seminars,
demonstrations, and tasting experiences. The Food & Wine festival
represents the best restaurants and chefs from Texas to D.C. and all
the states in between. Tickets for the Atlanta Food & Wine Festival
range from $75 for select Tasting Tents to the $2,500 Connoisseur
Package, which includes access to the exclusive Connoisseur Track,
Connoisseur Lounge and Events, Opening Reception, Tasting Tents,
the Street Cart Pavilion, and even early access to all seminars and
demonstrations.

Cinco de Mayo Block Party—Va-Hi (www.atlantacincodemayo
.com). This festival is held on Cinco de Mayo (May 5) each year.
The celebration and block party begins in the early evening
at Pozolé restaurant in the Virginia Highland neighborhood
(1044 Greenwood Ave. Northeast, Atlanta, 30306; (404)
892-0552). There is live music all evening. A $5 cover gets
guests into the celebration. Food and drink specials can
also be found at this festival. Not for children.

Marietta Greek Festival (www.mariettagreekfestival.org). Lesser known than the **Atlanta Greek Festival** (see p. xxiv), the Marietta Greek Festival takes place 4 months earlier at the Holy Transfiguration Greek Orthodox Church and attracts quite a crowd as well. The festival includes authentic Greek food like souvlaki, gyros, and, of course, baklava for dessert. Throughout the day there is live music and dancing. Dancers vary in age from quite young (kindergarten level) to young adults and are outfitted in Greek clothing. There is actually a Greek coliseum on church grounds that allows great views of the dancers. This in itself is a pretty spectacular sight. Don't miss the church tour, which is less than 30 minutes; you'll get to see the beautiful architecture and design in a small group. Admission is only $2.

Taste of Alpharetta (www.alpharetta.ga.us). Although somewhat unusual, the Taste of Alpharetta takes place on a Thursday evening—one day only in downtown Alpharetta at Wills Park. Over 50 restaurants participate. Sample appetizers, entrees, and desserts from the top restaurants in Alpharetta. The Taste of Alpharetta also includes culinary demonstrations, activities, and entertainment. Admission is free, but food samples are priced from $1 to $3. Tip: To get the best selection of food, arrive early as food goes fast. Parking can be difficult, so arrive as soon as possible to ensure good parking.

Taste of Marietta (www.tasteofmarietta.com). Taste of Marietta has been drawing an increasingly bigger crowd each year to this festival that occurs in late spring. Held on 1 day only (Sunday), over 70 restaurants participate. There is live music all day long and lots of entertainment for the kids as well: multiple moonwalks and games, sand art, face painting, and more! Moonwalks and some other activities have a nominal fee. Admission is free but tastes range from $1 to $4. Free parking is available in many of the nearby Cobb County government building parking decks.

Taste of the Nation (http://strength.org/ atlantataste). Taste of the Nation takes place at the Georgia Aquarium. Over the course of an evening, guests enjoy wines and tasty dishes from more than 50 top Atlanta restaurants, all for a good cause—to help end childhood hunger. Taste of the Nation has been in Atlanta for over a decade. General admission is $250 for the gala that goes from 7:30 to 10:00 p.m. VIP ticket purchasers ($350 per person) enter at 6:30 p.m. for the preview party.

Taste of Sandy Springs (www.tasteofsandysprings.org). Usually held on a Saturday afternoon, Taste of Sandy Springs features around 25 restaurants from the Sandy Springs area. Unlike other "Taste of" events, admission is not free; cost is $5. The "taste tickets" are $1 apiece, and tastes range from $1 to $3 each. A Gourmet Market with gourmet food products is a recent addition. The Green Market allows attendees to take home a selection of fresh Georgia-grown products. The event also offers a kids' activity village with interactive games and culinary art projects. There is also a silent auction to bid on restaurant meals, accommodations, and other entertainment items.

June

Virginia-Highland Summerfest (www.vahi.org/summerfest .html). The Virginia-Highland Summerfest takes place along Virginia Avenue in the heart of the Virginia-Highland neighborhood. Summerfest includes arts, foods, and live music and is a great event for the whole family. For the children, there is Kidsfest with lots of activities.

August

Corks and Forks Festival (www.gpconservancy.org/node/18). The Corks and Forks Festival is an opportunity to meet some local Atlanta chefs and sample their food. The festival encourages people to enjoy the century-old trees in historic Grant Park. There is a 5K run on Saturday morning and an Artist Market as well as live entertainment. For kids there is a Fun Center. Taste some great wines and ales from Atlanta's top restaurants. Tickets are $35, and each ticket is good for 1 day.

Pigs & Peaches BBQ Festival (www.facebook.com/PigsAnd Peaches). Taking place in Kennesaw, the Pigs & Peaches BBQ Festival is a 2-day festival that has garnered a tremendous following.

There is barbecue for sale from different vendors, a barbecue cook-off, and even a farmers' market. Besides food for sale, there is free music from a number of local and national acts, a large Kid Zone, and other exhibits with unique products for sale.

September

Atlanta Greek Festival (www.atlantagreekfestival.org). Taking place in late September, the Atlanta Greek Festival is a weekend-long celebration that draws in people from all over the Greater Atlanta area, held at the Greek Orthodox Cathedral. Besides traditional Greek food, entertainment includes Greek dancing, and inside the Greek church, artists sell their goods and jewelry. Entry is $5 for adults and $3 for children. Purchase online for a small discount.

October

Taste of Atlanta (www.tasteofatlanta.com). An all-encompassing food festival, the Taste of Atlanta draws food lovers from all over the Southeast. The festival showcases the diverse food and restaurants in Atlanta, and foodies gather to sample an enormous amount of tastes from more than 70 restaurants. There is also live entertainment and special cooking demos. Regular admission is $25 and includes 15 taste tickets. Tastes average 2 to 4 tickets each. In addition to regular admission, there's also a special VIP area of tasting tents and a beer-and-wine tent. VIP packages are $75. Kids 13 and under get in free with each paid adult admission.

Buckhead

For many years Buckhead sparkled by day as the swanky spot for shopping, working, and socializing. At night it drew in the younger crowd with a myriad of bars that young professionals flocked to. While there are still many skyscrapers and ultraposh boutiques, the post-college nightlife scene has been transformed to many more restaurants and condos. The "Buckhead Betties" or "ladies who lunch," as many refer to them, are still found around town at the upscale eateries. Many conventioneers prefer to stay in the Buckhead area versus Downtown because it has numerous restaurants that are easily accessible and within walking distance of hotels. As Buckhead evolves and changes, one thing remains constant: It will long be the epitome of Atlanta with its modern look and feel but friendly and distinctly Southern charm.

Amuse, 560 Dutch Valley Rd., Atlanta, GA 30324; (404) 888-1890; www.amuseatlanta.com; French/American; $$. Amuse is located in Piedmont Park but a little off the beaten path. During the warm months, you'll definitely want to take advantage of Amuse's inviting patio. But even if you choose to sit indoors, you'll be able to take advantage of the sky-line views with the floor-to-ceiling windows. The cuisine is French inspired; think of it as French food for the newbie. Escargot is on the menu, but a decent steak can be found there as well. A decidedly French entree is the *casserole du pêcheur,* or fisherman's stew, with mussels, scallops, and shrimp. Brunch features a *croque monsieur* or *croque madame.* Note that the restaurant is closed on Monday.

Annie's Thai Castle, 3195 Roswell Rd., Atlanta, GA 30305; (404) 264-9546; www.anniesthaicastle.com; Thai; $$. This authentic Thai restaurant has been around for years in the main drag of Buckhead. The bars may have come and gone, but Annie's remains with the same consistently good service, and the owner (Annie) remembers name and faces. Start things off with the coconut chicken soup. If you are looking for a light dish, go for the yum-yai or the Thai sausage salad. Any of the curries are notable entrees to try, and *pad kee mao* (drunken noodles) and the *pad prikh king* (chicken or beef) are exceptional entrees that shouldn't be missed. Friendly staff are happy to swap meat entrees with tofu. There is a private lot in back for parking.

The Big Ketch, 3279 Roswell Rd., Atlanta, GA 30305; (404) 474-9508; www.thebigketch.com; Seafood; $$. A somewhat new entrant into the Atlanta dining scene, the Big Ketch made quite a splash. Star starters include the ahi tuna and crab fritter appetizers. The hush puppies are amazing and worth ordering, even if you've never been a fan: They are nice and crispy on the outside and soft on the inside. Tip: For those watching calories, they offer a menu of low-calorie cocktails. Free parking.

Bistro Niko, 3344 Peachtree Rd., Atlanta, GA 30319; (404) 261-6456; www.buckheadrestaurants.com; French; $$$. Another restaurant that is part of the famed and very popular Buckhead Life Restaurant Group, this is truly a beautiful dining space. Entering the restaurant, you'll pass by the open kitchen, which showcases their beautiful meats in a glass display case. The colorful and well-appointed decor makes for an enjoyable lunch or dinner, and you'll find the place buzzing during both occasions. Start with the piquillo peppers stuffed with cod and potatoes, the ravioli, or the smoked salmon sandwiches. If you are trying to eat light, any of these are good options for a small meal. Not-to-miss entrees are the fried shrimp or duck. While the menu lends itself to romantic dining, bear in mind that the dining area is large and quite loud. So if a quiet, intimate evening is what you are seeking, you probably won't find it here. Great for business meetings, though. Reservations are a must.

Bluefin, 1261 W. Paces Ferry Rd. Northwest, Atlanta, GA 30327; (404) 963-5291; www.bluefinatlanta.com; Sushi; $$. Billed as a Japanese fusion sushi bar, the look is clean and minimalist, as is typical of sushi bars. There is a lot of white on the walls and modern-looking lighting fixtures. Tip: This is a great Buckhead lunch spot. There is free parking in the rear, and a great lunch can be had for around $10. Standout sushi rolls are Noran Tornado and the Last Samurai (nice take on the spicy tuna). If you are a crawfish lover, you won't want to miss the Hurricane roll.

Bluepointe, 3455 Peachtree Rd. Northeast, Atlanta, GA 30326; (404) 237-2060; www.buckheadrestaurants.com; Asian; $$$. Another gem from the Buckhead Life Restaurant Group, Bluepointe is part bar, part sushi joint, part high-end fusion restaurant. Notable entrees include the salmon with kumquat miso and the coconut curry lobster. There is a happy hour Monday through Thursday from 5 to 7 p.m. This includes $5 drinks (don't miss the apple martini) and half-price appetizers. Tip: Tuesday nights seem to turn the bar area into somewhat of a pickup place.

Brio, 2964 Peachtree Rd. Northwest, Atlanta, GA 30305; (404) 601-5555; www.brioitalian.com; Italian; $$$. Brio is an Italian eatery that is perfect for a romantic date or good for group dining. Drinks are great and reasonably priced under $10. Don't miss the brus-chetta specials. They have different toppings that are changed out, but all are exceptional, including items like prosciutto, asparagus, and mozzarella. Tip: Great bar specials here during the week. Many of their appetizers are under $3 during happy hour. Surprisingly their burger is quite tasty, too!

Bucket Shop, 3475 Lenox Rd. Northeast, #220, Atlanta, GA 30326; (404) 261-9244; www.bucketshopcafe.com; American; $$. This Buckhead bar has been around for quite some time and is extremely popular for its patio. The food is primarily bar food—(wings, mozzarella sticks, burgers). One of the nice things is that there is a big parking deck with lots of spaces so you don't have to mess with a valet or street parking. Arriving in town late and looking for something other than hotel food? Head to this prime Buckhead spot for decent bar food; out-of-towners appreciate that they can get bar food here late at night. This is the place to go for college football viewing! Menu highlights: burgers, Jack Daniel's wings.

Buckhead Bottle Bar, 268 E. Paces Ferry Rd., Atlanta, GA 30305; (404) 474-9892; www.buckheadbottlebar.com; American; $$. The name suggests more of a bar than a restaurant, but note that this place does serve up food in a pretty atmosphere. The tables have lights inside them that make the decor rather attractive. If you are looking for a quiet ambience, get there early as this definitely turns into a bar with louder music as the evening wears on. On the upside, if you are looking for dinner and a place to hang out afterward, this has the atmosphere for both. The lamb burger with goat cheese and ahi tuna salad are particularly good menu items. Tip: Fun people watching. There's a rooftop patio that gets hopping on weekends with a 20-something crowd.

Cafe Agora, 262 E. Paces Ferry Rd. Northeast, Atlanta, GA 30305; (404) 949-0900; www.cafeagora.com; Mediterranean; $$. This Turkish/Mediterranean restaurant is located in the middle of all the Buckhead action. Although Cafe Agora has been around for quite a while and garnered a pretty loyal following, they haven't expanded; the restaurant has only 8 to 10 tables. Most patrons get their food to go. However, it is a great spot if you are dining alone. The meze plate is the perfect start, allowing for a sampling of the most popular items. You'll be treated to dolmas (stuffed grape leaves), hummus, baba ghanoush, tabbouleh, and *hvuc ezme* (a carrot salad). The gyro is not to be missed; it's big enough to feed two people. Parking can be difficult. There isn't a lot on-site, so you'll have to find a nearby lot for parking.

Cellar 56, 56 E. Andrews Dr., Atlanta, GA 30305; (404) 869-1132; www.cellar56.com; Tapas; $$$. There are 56 different wine choices, hence the name. Or is it the address? This is a perfect date spot. You'll walk through a beautiful courtyard before entering the cozy but well-appointed restaurant. Bottles of wine line the walls of its interior. The focus is as much on the food as the wine here. Although a tapas menu, it is carefully thought out as opposed to offering countless options. It is divided into four parts: garden, land, sea, and sweets. A fair gauge is to allow 3 tapas per person. Start with the crab avocado salad and the duck confit flatbread, complete with fig jam—it will steal your heart. A must-try is the mac 'n' cheese; the creamy shell pasta is mixed with prosciutto and green chiles, for the perfect amount of spice and slightly salty flavor. The flatiron steak is perfect for sharing as well; with the chimichurri and arugula, it is another standout menu item. Tips: Two-for-one Tuesday; BOGO tapas plates.

Coast Seafood, 111 W. Paces Ferry Rd., Atlanta, GA 30305; (404) 869-0777; www.h2sr.com/coast; Seafood; $$$. In the warmer months, take advantage of the large patio of this casual seafood eatery. They're known for their oysters, and the mignonette sauce is especially good. Try anything crab and you can't go wrong—crab fritters, crab legs, crab summer roll. For a side, you must try their mac 'n' cheese; the creamy dish served up with bacon is very tasty and filling. The atmosphere is great for groups or a girls' night out. Tip: They have a large, fun patio perfect for sitting back and enjoying drinks and dinner with friends.

Dantanna's, 3400 Around Lenox Rd. Northeast, Atlanta, GA 30326; (404) 760-8873; www.dantannas.com; American; $$$. Dantanna's is

Specialty Nights in Atlanta

Buckhead Bottle Bar (see p. 5). This trendy bar in Buckhead offers all you can eat small bites for $10 every Tuesday. Some samples of food offerings are fried calamari, crab-and-cheese fritters, and crispy chicken tenders.

La Tavola (see p. 75). Molto Monday at La Tavola is the best pasta deal in Atlanta. Choose from 3 different pasta specials that evening, and add to that all the fresh bread you can eat for only $10. Menu offerings have included carbonara and lamb sausage lasagna.

Serpas True Food (see p. 72). On Sunday evening, Serpas has a special Sunday Supper dinner. This is a 3-course dinner for $20 for adults and $9 for children. The meal starts with a soup or salad, followed by an entree, which is then paired with sides, all served family style. The last course is dessert. Entrees could include steak, trout, or chicken breast.

a prime choice for after-work or happy hour gatherings with your coworkers and pals. There are lots of TVs for sports watching. While the steak varieties are plenty, the wasabi tuna topped with lump crab and the cioppino (lobster, crab, shrimp, mussels, and clams in a tomato broth) will make seafood lovers happy. There are also 50 wines available by the glass. Tip: While most people visit after

The Shed at Glenwood (475 Bill Kennedy Way, Atlanta, GA 30316; 404-835-4363; www.theshedatglenwood.com). This modern American restaurant features two weekly specials worth noting. First is the $3 slider night on Wednesday. The chef creates more than ten sliders each Wednesday, and all these sliders are only $3. This could include scallop, veal Parmesan, pork schnitzel, lamb meatball, pork belly, or Reuben, just to name a few. Not a meat eater? On Thursday they offer a vegetable plate (pick 4 vegetables) for $10. Standouts are sunchokes, onion rings, and asparagus.

Twist and **Shout** (Twist: 3500 Peachtree Rd. Northeast, Atlanta, GA 30326; Shout: 1197 Peachtree St. Northeast, Atlanta 30361; www.h2sr.com). These are sister restaurants that serve American food with an Asian flair. The best dishes are small plates or tapas. On Monday they offer all-you-can-eat tapas for $10.

work or for dinner, Dantanna's also serves up a pretty solid brunch. Options include Fried Oysters Rockefeller and Shirred Eggs in Tulips (2 eggs baked in crepes with Maine lobster, shrimp, and crawfish).

Dante's Down the Hatch, 3380 Peachtree Rd., Atlanta, GA 30326; (404) 266-1600; www.dantesdownthehatch.com; Fondue; $$$$.

Who's down for some fondue on a pirate ship surrounded by alligators? If you are, then you should head to Dante's. The restaurant has remained a popular destination for out-of-towners and those looking to have a romantic evening. This is the kind of restaurant where the atmosphere and ambience are meant to be taken in slowly, so don't plan to have a quick meal and scoot to a movie. And what is fondue if you don't have chocolate fondue, right? Note: If you would like to have chocolate fondue, you need a reservation at least two days in advance and a party of at least 6. Reservations are a must. It's $9 extra per person to sit on the ship.

Henri's Bakery, 61 Irby Ave. Northwest, Atlanta, GA 30305; (404) 237-0202; www.henrisbakery.com; Bakery; $. Henri's has been an Atlanta institution for 80 years. Great spot to grab a sandwich and go. They also offer a wide variety of pastries and desserts—nearly 40 different kinds of pastries to choose from. The tuna sandwich and po'boys (beef or turkey) are fantastic. They also cater and offer boxed lunches, so it's perfect if you need to pick up lunch for the office.

HOBNOB, 1551 Piedmont Ave., Atlanta, GA 30324; (404) 968-2288; www.hobnobatlanta.com; Pub; $$$. Hobnob has an English pub feel to it, although it's hip and trendy at the same time. This neighborhood pub, very popular with those living in close proximity, offers indoor seating with cozy tables or outdoor seating featuring multiple decks. The beer list is extensive and has many options on draft or by the bottle. The endive boats with figs and goat cheese, prosciutto, and Tabasco honey are the perfect mix of sweet, salty, crunchy, and spicy. Another unique and tasty starter is the Southern spring rolls with pork, collards, and a cherry-mustard marmalade: You won't find this on the menu at many restaurants. You can't go wrong with the fish-and-chips entree: The three large pieces of fish are crispy on the outside and tender and flaky on the inside, just how they should be. This seems the type of place where a group of friends might meet for drinks. And although they are open late, it has much more of a dinner crowd. Reservations are a must.

Kaleidoscope, 1410 Dresden Dr., Ste. 100, Atlanta, GA 30319; (404) 474-9600; www.k-pub.com; Pub; $$$. A neighborhood pub just slightly north of Buckhead in the Brookhaven community, Kaleidoscope draws a crowd of neighborhood residents and foodies who venture out for tasty and out-of-the-ordinary items. The menu is diverse in that it includes inexpensive starters, small plates, and full-blown entrees for those who want to indulge in a myriad of flavors. Start things off with the pork pot stickers. Kaleidoscope won best burger at a recent burger contest. Their award-winning burger, piled with pimiento cheese and chow chow, is a standout, as is the true Southern classic, shrimp 'n' grits. The mahimahi tostada is another winner in the entree department, with its smoked tomato and feta cheese topping. Beer lovers will appreciate the selection of craft beers. The noise level is reasonable, so although it is considered a pub, you can quite easily carry on a conversation without yelling. On the weekends it does get crowded, so if visiting on a Friday or Saturday night, be prepared to wait for a table as they do not take reservations; however, they do take call-ahead seating.

La Grotta, 2637 Peachtree Rd., Atlanta, GA 30305; (404) 231-1368; www.lagrottaatlanta.com; Italian; $$$$. Though the clientele is very mature—late 50s and 60s—the Italian food is phenomenal. Italian classics are served by a staff that offers superior service. Surprisingly, it is located in the basement of an apartment complex but rather than feeling dingy, it feels like you've stumbled upon a secret gem. The decor is a bit dated, so those desiring a trendy look should dine elsewhere. Start with the carpaccio, calamari, mussels, or the prosciutto appetizers. Risotto is creamy and rich, and veal scaloppine and other veal dishes are standouts, as are fish entrees. Tip: They regularly offer a "stimulus" menu with appetizer, entree, and a glass of wine for under $25. Reservations required.

Local Three, 3290 Northside Pkwy., Ste. 120, Atlanta, GA 30327; (404) 968-2700; www.localthree.com; Gastropub; $$. A hot spot on the Atlanta dining scene, Local Three completely renovated the previous space and created a warm and inviting pub-style restaurant. Their slogan is "Sit Deep and Stay Awhile," which they truly mean. The servers are both friendly and knowledgeable about the upscale Southern menu. The farm-to-table food is sophisticated without being pretentious. For starters, the Meat Butter (or chicken liver mousse) is phenomenal, and the brussels sprouts put aside any previous doubts about them being anything but tasty. The charcuterie plate aptly named Notorious P.I.G. is perfect to share with dining companions. The chicken potpie and lobster roll sandwich are other choice menu items. Note the menu changes daily depending on what is in season and what is available, as owners aim to make this completely farm-to-table dining. Park in the garage next door and bring your receipt in to be validated. Sunday brunch is offered as well with true Southern favorites. Reservations strongly encouraged. Tip: Each Monday at 7 p.m. a 3-course meal with beer/wine pairings is available for $35 per person plus tax and tip.

Nakato Japanese Restaurant, 1776 Cheshire Bridge Rd., Atlanta, GA 30324; (404) 873-6582; www.nakatorestaurant.com; Japanese; $$$. If you want to enjoy Japanese hibachi in a non-chain restaurant, Nakato is the place to visit. The staff is friendly and helpful, and the hibachi chefs are funny and love posing for pictures. Hibachi choices are a standard combination of two of the following: shrimp, chicken, steak, and scallops. Sushi is also on the menu, if it's preferred. The negihama roll, with yellowtail and green onion, is simple yet full of taste and texture. The white kelp roll contains a stuffing of chopped crab tempura, green onions, caviar, and aioli, wrapped in white kelp. The large seating areas, especially the hibachi tables, are a terrific option for a birthday celebration with a large group. Tip: Try the happy hour special available Monday through Friday from 5:30 to 6:30 p.m. Choose a cocktail and 5 small plates for only $15. Items include calamari, spicy tuna roll, panko shrimp, seafood roll, and pork dumplings. Parking is valet only.

Nino's, 1931 Cheshire Bridge Rd. Northeast, Atlanta, GA 30324; (404) 874-6505; www.ninosatlanta.com; Italian; $$$$. Nino's is rather small but very cozy. Another restaurant that has been in Atlanta for decades, it serves up authentic Italian cuisine. Their bruschetta, escargot, and calamari are all pretty tasty. A signature starter that shouldn't be missed is the melon with prosciutto—very fresh. The lasagna is classic and the ultimate comfort food at Nino's: It overflows with cheesy goodness and is filled with meat. As one would expect, the selection of wines by the glass is very solid. Servers tout veal dishes, but seafood dishes are every bit as good, if not better. After your meal, they'll bring the dessert cart by, so don't forget to save room as many desserts are dreamy and made in-house. Tiramisu, coconut cake, and Bailey's cheesecake are just some of the desserts worth mentioning. Note: Although in the Buckhead area, this side of town is slightly seedy (read: neon-lit gentleman's clubs).

Portofino, 3199 Paces Ferry Place Northwest, Atlanta, GA 30305; (404) 231-1136; www.portofinobistro.com; Mediterranean; $$$. Portofino is tucked away from the main drag of Buckhead. No matter—it still has a lively crowd, especially on weekends. Ladies should note the stone walkway into the restaurant can be tricky if wearing heels. Inside, the tables are set close together in this renovated house. The noise level can get quite high when it's busy, so it might not be the best setting for a romantic date on a Saturday night. The short-rib bruschetta appetizer should not be missed: The bread is piled high and heavy with meat. The fried artichokes are a solid vegetarian choice served up with a tarragon aioli. The veal scaloppine with prosciutto, sage, and tomato is a filling and delicious meal with flavors that marry well together. On the lighter side the shrimp and eggplant pappardelle is another highlight. The pasta, made daily by a local vendor, tastes house-made. Valet parking is $5, but nearby street or lot parking can be found quite easily. Reservations required. Note: Even with reservations, patio seating is first come, first serve.

Sheik Burritos and Kabobs, 1877 Piedmont Rd., Atlanta, GA 30324; (404) 815-0227; http://sheikburritos.com; Burritos; $. While the whole Korean taco craze seems to be going strong, these are slightly different: a mix of Persian and Tex-Mex. Think Middle East meets Southwest. Located in a nondescript strip mall on the outskirts of Buckhead, they offer up some creative burrito concoctions. Sheik also offers several different kinds of dip-and-chip starters. Traditional salsa and guacamole are two of them, but the hummus and baba ghanoush are offered as well. El Kosher-Halal burrito, with Berkshire pork, raisins, pistachios, mint, apples, eggplant, and lentils is a winner, as is La Dirka-Dirka burrito made with lamb, spicy sauce with tomatoes and eggplants, basmati rice, beets, feta, and spinach. For those craving a more traditional burrito, the El Bandido Border Patrol contains chicken, black beans, and salsa wrapped in a flour tortilla. All sauces and dips are made in-house, and meats are organic. In fact, the menu is almost entirely organic and almost all gluten-free as well.

Souper Jenny, 56 E. Andrews Dr. Northwest, Ste. 22, Atlanta, GA 30305; (404) 239-9023; www.souperjennyatl.com; Sandwiches/ Soups; $. The decor is eclectic. The varieties of soups change daily so as not to bore anyone. The turkey chili is one of the most popular menu items. Other soups that are favored are the gazpacho, cucumber (served cold), and chicken tortilla. They offer a soup, sandwich, soda, and cookie for $12. It does get crowded in the restaurant, so many patrons choose to get their orders to go. Tip: Try to visit during off-peak times as parking can be hard to find. Also, credit cards are not accepted, so bring cash. Tuesday and Thursday grilled cheese nights are popular with families.

Taka Sushi, 385 Pharr Rd., Atlanta, GA 30305; (404) 869-2802; www.takasushiatlanta.com; Sushi; $$$. Tucked away in a strip mall, Taka remains a favorite for those looking for stellar sushi in Buckhead. Taka plays homage to some of Atlanta's hometown companies, featuring rolls like the Home Depot Roll, Diet Coke Roll, and UPS and CNN Rolls. For those seeking variety and a tasting of many different items, opt for the 8-course *omakase* (chef's choice) menu. One of the menu highlights is the *hamachi kami* (yellowtail cheek); there are only a couple available every day, but it is prepared excellently and is very meaty. If you really want it, call in advance to reserve it. Another highlight is the live scallop, which is alive when sliced and served up with kiwi, lemon, and herbs. Service is on point, with servers able to make suggestions and happy to bring sake samples to taste. For drinks, choose from 30-plus wines and premium sake from their *Wine Spectator* award-winning list. Closed on Sunday.

Tantra, 2285 Peachtree Rd., Ste. 100, Atlanta, GA 30309; (404) 228-7963; www.tantraatlanta.com; Asian; $$$$. Asian fusion restaurant Tantra serves up tasty cocktails in a beautiful, well-appointed dining area. The Buddha painting and the Tantric chair are just two of the items that help build on the Asian theme here. The bartenders, managers, and servers are all proud of the cocktail menu, which they each helped concoct. The Tantric cocktail with gin, elderflower, thyme, and lime juice is a refreshing kickoff to the meal. Start with the hummus tasting—a combination of chickpea, edamame, and truffle, each one is distinctive and has its own appeal. *Foie gras* aficionados will enjoy Tantra's take served with a spiced apple chutney. The scallops and pomegranate-braised short ribs are favorites, but the ostrich is probably the tastiest menu item; when prepared medium, its surprising beefy flavor comes through perfectly. Definitely order a side of cauliflower, which has a unique, slightly nutty taste.

Valenza, 1441 Dresden Dr., Ste. 100, Atlanta, GA 30319; (404) 969-3233; www.valenzarestaurant.com; Italian; $$$. Along with its sister restaurant, **Haven** (p. 25), Valenza is located in the Brookhaven area and frequented by the many residents of the Brookhaven community. They do have a solid wine selection, but note that they make their own limoncello in-house, so a cocktail that contains this won't disappoint. The mussels, which are also available at Haven, are a standout: garlicky with chunks of tomatoes. For mains the risotto is prepared creamy and al dente, just as it should be. Vegetarians and nonvegetarians can both appreciate the butternut squash ravioli with its pecans, brown butter, and sage. The pork saltimbocca is a no-brainer: Pork tenderloin, prosciutto, broccoli—it is tender, juicy, and tasty. Service is very attentive here. Valenza is very popular in the community and goes above and beyond to ensure that guests' needs are met, including any special dietary restrictions. The restaurant works well for a cozy date or a girls' night out and is regularly host to birthday celebrations. Tip: Monday night is half off wine bottles.

Landmarks

Alfredo's, 1989 Cheshire Bridge Rd., Atlanta, GA 31136; www.alfredositalianrestaurant.com; Italian; $$$. A landmark in Atlanta for over 30 years, you can smell the garlic wafting out into the parking lot when you arrive. Inside you'll find low lighting, red vinyl booths, and waiters with thick Italian accents. For appetizers, don't miss out on the melon with prosciutto di Parma. Lasagna, beef cannelloni, snapper *Francese,* and shrimp scampi are menu highlights. If you are a coffee drinker, end your dinner with the cappuccino. Reservations are a must.

Anis, 2974 Grandview Ave. Northeast, Atlanta, GA 30305; (404) 233-9889; www.anisbistro.com; French; $$$. Another French restaurant located in Buckhead, this one also has a lovely patio. It blends chic and sophistication at the same time. You'll feel as if you were invited into a good friend's house for a meal, not some stuffy restaurant. As this is French don't miss out on the *moules marinières*—mussels in garlicky, buttery sauce. Steak's a hit, but any fish—trout or halibut—doesn't disappoint. On weekend evenings they have live music, but it complements the dining experience and is not overly loud as some restaurant music can be. It is worth mentioning again that the patio is lovely; opt for sitting here whenever possible.

Aria, 490 E. Paces Ferry Rd. Northeast, Atlanta, GA 30305; (404) 233-7673; www.aria-atl.com; American; $$$$. An elegant and classy establishment, Aria has been a Buckhead fixture for years. The white linens and walls are a stark contrast to the dark floor and ceiling, but they add up to beautiful surroundings; a one-of-a-kind ornate lighting fixture hangs above the main dining room. This is a romantic place for couples or double dates (think anniversary celebrations). Start with the *foie gras* with vanilla-glazed Fuji apple and arugula or the lobster cocktail, which is served in a martini glass, as you may expect, with mashed potatoes. The beef short rib is one of the most flavorful and tender you'll find anywhere. Chef-Owner Gerry Klaskala is extremely focused on the farm-to-table movement, which is evident in the menu.

Atlanta Fish Market, 265 Pharr Rd. Northeast, Atlanta, GA 30305; (404) 262-3165; www.buckheadrestaurants.com; Seafood; $$$$. Part of the Buckhead Life Restaurant Group, you can't miss this restaurant—it is the one that has the big fish atop the roof. Upon entering, your eyes will feast on the beautiful display of fish in the ice case. Sushi is preva-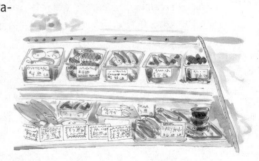lent on the menu, although it isn't a sushi restaurant per se. This is the kind of restaurant that presents classic seafood dishes—clam chowder, stuffed flounder, lobster tails, and more. The options aren't new or trendy but more tried and true. There are many seafood choices and lots of fresh fish can be found. Reservations are a must, even on weeknights.

Blue Ridge Grill, 1261 W. Paces Ferry Rd. Northwest, Atlanta, GA 30327; (404) 233-5030; www.blueridgegrill.com; American; $$$. An

Atlanta classic, the Blue Ridge Grill has been around for decades. The interior resembles an upscale log cabin, and the name pays homage to the Blue Ridge Mountains in North Georgia. Think wood on the walls but white tablecloths in dark wood booths. Some of the signature items are the Georgia trout and horseradish-crusted grouper. Meat lovers will enjoy the 20-ounce rib eye. The dinner and lunch menus are almost identical, so if you are looking to spend less or want to sample Blue Ridge Grill but want to try other area restaurants, too, visit at lunch and you won't miss anything. Tip: If you visit for brunch you'll be tempted to fill up on the hot buns, but refrain and allow room for your main meal. The downstairs features a private dining area that can fit up to 45 people.

Bone's, 3130 Piedmont Rd. Northeast, Atlanta, GA 30305; (404) 237-2663; www.bonesrestaurant.com; Steaks; $$$$. This well-established restaurant has been an Atlanta institution for over 30 years. As the name may suggest, this is a steak house, and a high-end one at that. Don't expect trendy here, but do expect exceptional service and steaks. Great for groups, and the seafood platter with crab, jumbo shrimp, and lobster is perfect to share. Beef carpaccio is a notable starter. The New York strip is probably the most popular and best steak on the menu.

Buckhead Diner, 3073 Piedmont Rd., Atlanta, GA 30305; (404) 262-3336; www.buckheadliferestaurants.com; American; $$$. The neon glow and shiny chrome exterior scream "diner," but put aside any notions you have of a typical diner, as this isn't your

TOP CHEF ALUMNI

Throughout the seasons of the popular television show *Top Chef,* Atlanta has been represented by some very talented chefs. Atlantans have been supportive of our skilled chefs and have made sure that they continue to thrive in the city by patronizing their restaurants. Some of these chefs have gone on to open several restaurants in the Atlanta area and have enjoyed lots of success due to the support from patrons.

Richard Blais

Probably the most famous Atlanta *Top Chef* contestant, Richard Blais won *Top Chef: All Stars* in 2011 after coming in second in *Top Chef* season four. Blais is known for putting his own personal style on traditional fine cuisine. He opened the hotter-than-hot restaurant **Flip Burger** (see p. 90). These gourmet burgers are served in a fun and lively atmosphere. Flip has two locations: one in Buckhead and the original in the trendy West Midtown area. Fun facts about Blais: He thinks everyone should keep duck fat in their pantry. He also was inspired to become a chef after working at McDonald's as a teen; he found the camaraderie in the kitchen to be very energetic and pleasing and knew he wanted to make food his career.

Tracey Bloom

Tracey Bloom had a brief run on *Top Chef* in season eight. She has spent much time at top restaurants in Atlanta, including 103 West in Buckhead, Sia's, and Table 1280 in Midtown. She is now chef at **Ray's Killer Creek** (see p. 191) in Alpharetta. Although the menu consists of mostly steaks, Chef Bloom has brought in her own style, introducing a selection of flatbreads like prosciutto and arugula, house-made pastas, and a savory short rib.

Kevin Gillespie

One of the consistently top-rated restaurants in town is Kevin Gillespie's **Woodfire Grill** (see p. 31). Located in Buckhead, Woodfire Grill is a rather small restaurant tucked into a slightly seedy area of town, but that doesn't stop the loyal fans of Kevin Gillespie. His restaurant features locally sourced items, and the menu changes regularly to accommodate new ingredients. Guests rave about his 5- and 7-course tasting menus; the small courses pack in creative and delicious flavors.

Eli Kirshtein

Eli Kirshtein, who started working in kitchens at the young age of 16, shared the stage with Kevin Gillespie and Hector Santiago in season six of *Top Chef.* He has also worked under the direction of Chef Kevin Rathbun and another *Top Chef* alumnus, Richard Blais. At the time he was chef at the popular Atlanta restaurant Eno, which has since closed. He has stayed busy appearing at cooking demonstrations around the country. Most recently he played a big role in the organization of food trucks for the Atlanta Food & Wine Festival.

Hector Santiago

After a brief stint on *Top Chef* in season six, Chef Santiago didn't let that slow him down. His wildly popular restaurant **Pura Vida** (see p. 76) serves Latin tapas, melding unique flavors together. Think mahimahi with banana, or tofu seviche. The result is a restaurant like no other. Since leaving *Top Chef*, Chef Santiago added another restaurant to his pedigree: El Burro Pollo, a sandwich shop.

average one. Part of the Buckhead Life Restaurant Group, the food is upscale, and servers don jackets. Maytag blue cheese chips are one of the best starters on the menu. Comfort food like burgers and fries are wonderful,. Fish lovers shouldn't miss out on the mahimahi tostada. Don't forget to save room for dessert. The Key lime pie and James Beard Award–winning banana cream pie, while not the most inventive, are fabulous. (When Giada de Laurentiis visited she declared that she loved their banana cream pie.) Note: They don't take reservations, but it is recommended that you make priority seating reservations through Open Table, an online reservations system (www .opentable.com), as wait times can be quite lengthy on weekends.

Chops, 70 W. Paces Ferry Rd. Northwest, Atlanta, GA 30305; (404) 262-2675; www.buckheadrestaurants.com; Steaks; $$$$. Another restaurant that is part of the Buckhead Life Restaurant Group, Chops is very classy and very pricey. Waiters wear jackets, and service here is impeccable. Many business outings are held here, and the noise level can get rather high; for a romantic date, a weekend evening would be a better time to visit. Start with the fried lobster tail served up with some honey mustard—this is perfection. For mains order the filet, New York strip, or the rib eye, but skip the Wagyu steak, very pricey at nearly a Benjamin ($100), but only marginally better tasting than other steaks. Side sauces such as béarnaise are optional, but the steaks are done perfectly and the addition of any sauce is unnecessary. Reservations are a must.

Colonnade, 1879 Cheshire Bridge Rd. Northeast, Atlanta, GA 30324; (404) 874-5642; www.colonnadeatl.com; Southern; $$. The Colonnade is a historic restaurant that has been around since the 1920s, featuring traditional Southern food. This is where you take out-of-town guests to sample Southern food. The decor is sorely in need of updating, but that is part of the charm of the restaurant. And if you are under the age of 65, you will probably be the youngest patron. Don't miss out on their fried chicken, fried pork chops, chicken livers, grits, or sweet tea. Sweet tea goes hand in hand with Southern food. This is the kind of place to indulge in fried foods, and desserts like the coconut cream pie. Colonnade has an early bird special for $11, which includes an entree, 2 sides, beverage, and dessert. It's available Mon through Thur 5 to 6:30 p.m., and Sat noon to 4 p.m. Note that they only take cash—no credit cards accepted.

Haven, 1441 Dresden Dr. Northeast, Atlanta, GA 30319; (404) 969-0700; www.havenrestaurant.com; American; $$$. Located very close to the hustle and bustle of Buckhead in the Brookhaven neighborhood, Haven is a restaurant adored by those who live in the area. Start with the crab cake and the mussels; although the menu does change with the seasons, these two always remain. For entrees, duck and pork are always prepared perfectly and in very large portions. Presentation and plating are absolutely gorgeous throughout, as if an artist plated up the food. The patio is gorgeous and should be taken advantage of on warm days. The interior is pretty as well, but can get very loud when crowded. Tip: On Tuesday they offer a burger and a glass of wine for $15.

Holeman & Finch, 2277 Peachtree Rd. Northeast, Atlanta, GA 30309; (404) 948-1175; www.holeman-finch.com; Gastropub; $$$. This hard-to-find gastropub has been wowing visitors with its coveted burger ever since it launched. There are no signs from the street (or even on the door) that confirm the name is actually Holeman & Finch. You just have to know where it is. Hint: If you can find **Restaurant Eugene** (p. 29), then you can find H&F. The space is rather small and gets crowded every night. The one communal table in the middle of the restaurant seats most patrons, and it's good that small plates are ordered commonly, as table space is at a premium. Ask your server to pick out a concoction for you, and you won't be disappointed. Some argue that this is the best burger in town; if you want to decide for yourself you must be there well before 10 p.m. to place your order. They only make 24 per day and serve them after 10 p.m., but if you can get there on a Sunday, they make a ton of them all day long. Other menu items are the charcuterie plate, and offal like fried pig's ears and veal sweetbreads. If you are traveling by yourself this is a fun place to go as it is rather easy to chat up other patrons.

Kyma, 3085 Piedmont Rd. Northeast, Atlanta, GA 30305; (404) 262-0702; www.buckheadrestaurants.com; Greek; $$$$. Yet another one of the Buckhead Life Restaurant Group, Kyma serves up contemporary Greek food in an upscale atmosphere. Service is stellar at all of the group's restaurants, but especially at Kyma. The decor is nothing short of stunning. Enter and see a constellation display on the deep blue ceiling and white marble columns reminiscent of Greek architecture. If you are looking for some of the freshest seafood with Greek seasoning, than Kyma is the spot to go. The octopus and dolmas (stuffed grape leaves) are great starters, as is the beef moussaka, which is like a meat pie layered with eggplant, kasseri cheese, and béchamel sauce. If you're with a group or wanting to sample small plates, take advantage of their appetizer special on Sunday when all appetizers are $7. Fish is the standout here. The selection isn't huge as they focus on a selection of top-notch varieties: The sole and barramundi are two of the best choices to be had. Don't miss out on the *loukoumades*—deep-fried doughnut balls soaked in a honey syrup—for dessert. There is a surprisingly wonderful kids' menu, too.

Nava, 3060 Peachtree Rd. Northwest, Ste. 160, Atlanta, GA 30305; (404) 240-1984; www.buckheadrestaurants.com; Southwestern; $$$$. Nava, part of the Buckhead Life Restaurant Group, is focused on upscale Southwestern food. The decor throughout the restaurant exudes a Southwestern authenticity the restaurant strives for. Nava is a favorite of celebrities and business travelers who visit Atlanta regularly. As this is a bit of a high-end restaurant, rather than presenting diners with chips and salsa, what you'll get is a very tasty blue corn bread. Nava does offer a salsa tasting for $5, which includes three of their house-made salsas: chipotle-tomatillo with cilantro, mango-habañero, and avocado-tomatillo with lime juice. Start things off with the prickly pear margarita. Menu highlights are the Pork Two Ways, which includes a tenderloin and a pork tamale with a habañero-peach glaze, and the lamb loin with cipollini onions and a tamarind-lime caramel sauce. Brunch options are fantastic as well: shrimp 'n' grits, Baja fish, and brisket tacos are tasty, as is the omelette with tequila sour cream, rojo mole, pico de gallo, and chorizo hash browns. Tip: For $18.95 get a starter, 2 tacos of your choosing and a side. Valet parking is $2. Gluten-free menu available. Reservations required.

OK Cafe, 1284 W. Paces Ferry Rd. Northwest, Atlanta, GA 30327; (404) 233-2888; www.okcafe.com; Breakfast/Brunch; $$. Located in the heart of Buckhead, this popular brunch spot is always hopping, and diners don't seem to mind the long waits for a table. Pancakes and omelettes are favorite menu items. Although they are known for their breakfast foods, there are also a lot of Southern foods on the menu: Think chicken fried steak, collard greens, and mac 'n' cheese. Portions are huge. The dining room is kitschy and the servers' uniforms are all old-school—like 1950s old-school. Complete your retro dining experience with a burger and a $5 milk shake (yes, they are wonderful and worth the money). Tip: Bypass the wait for a table and just sit at the counter. It is a freestanding building in a strip mall, so there is plenty of free parking all around.

Pricci, 500 Pharr Rd. Northeast, Atlanta, GA 30305; (404) 237-2941; www.buckheadrestaurants.com; Italian; $$$. Pricci is one of two Italian restaurants that is part of the Buckhead Life Restaurant Group. Although the dress code is stated as dressy, you can wear a nice pair of jeans and dressy shirt and do just fine. Don't miss the appetizer of warm bread with marinara and goat cheese dip. It is something regulars love and find extremely tasty. The melon and prosciutto is a highlight to start your meal. Tortelli filled with artichoke, spinach, and cacioricotta cheese with brown butter sauce and pine nuts pack a lot of flavor even if you are a meat eater. Other carnivores will enjoy the short rib ravioli or osso buco. Servers are well-versed in the menu and astute at recommending wine to complement your meal. For a leisurely lunch sit back and enjoy one of their panini or the arugula-topped prosciutto pizza.

Restaurant Eugene, 2277 Peachtree Rd. Northeast, Atlanta, GA 30309; (404) 355-0321; www.restauranteugene.com; Southern/American; $$$$. Restaurant Eugene is owned by Linton Hopkins, who named the establishment for his grandfather. Hopkins was named one of *Food & Wine* magazine's 2009 Best New Chefs and was a James Beard nominee for Best Chef Southeast in 2011. They are extremely big on the farm-to-table movement here. The food and top-notch service leave nothing to be desired, but it is very pricey.

This is the kind of place where you'll be blown away by the *amuse bouche* and keep being impressed as the meal goes on. Portions aren't huge, but the creativity and complexity of each dish make every bite worth the price tag. Start with the trout tartare; the grapefruit, vanilla, and peppers in it play off each other well and make for a tasty start. Melt-in-your-mouth salmon and crispy duck are two mains not to missed. For dessert, skip the traditional dessert options and go for the house-made sorbet or, if you are a cheese lover, order the cheese plate. Both 5- and 7-course tasting menus are offered.

10 Degrees South, 4183 Roswell Rd. Northeast, Atlanta, GA 30342; (404) 705-8870; www.10degreessouth.com; South African; $$$$. Opened in 1998, 10 Degrees South is the only South African restaurant in Atlanta (surprising, as we have so many Ethiopian restaurants). Situated off Roswell Road, 10 Degrees South is one of those charming, classy restaurants that, for whatever reason, stay under the radar in the Atlanta dining scene. The calamari is a must (this one is served up unfried) as are the *sosaties,* skewered beef in an apricot curry sauce. For something authentically South African, order the bobotie, a sweet ground-beef mixture topped with custard; think of it as South African shepherd's pie. Instead of peas, carrots, and other vegetables, this "pie" of sorts has apples, apricots, and raisins. As a side dish, the sambals are the South African version of grits. While there are items for nonadventurous eaters on the menu, it is worth exploring the unique food offerings, as they are all standouts. See 10 Degrees South's recipe for **Bobotie** on p. 228.

Varasano's Pizza, 2171 Peachtree Rd., Atlanta, GA 30309; (404) 352-8216; www.varasanos.com; Pizza; $$. Varasano's creator and owner, Jeff Varasano, a former techie, started making pizzas here in the Neapolitan way: cooking pizzas for only a couple minutes in a very high-temperature oven. An almost overnight sensation, Varasano's has had a loyal following of customers since opening. The menu is somewhat limited with only 9 pizzas to choose from, but patrons can build their own pizza by selecting ingredients of their choosing. Nana's, the house special, is the pizza Jeff's grand-mother used to make: topped with mozzarella and tomato sauce with a secret blend of Italian herbs. For something different, try the New Haven clam pizza: Made with clams, mussels, and garlic, it can be ordered with white or red sauce. Tip: Become a fan of Varasano's on Facebook and you'll be privy to the ongoing monthly specials.

Woodfire Grill, 1782 Cheshire Bridge Rd. Northeast, Atlanta, GA 30324; (404) 347-9055; www.woodfiregrill.com; American; $$$$. Owned by *Top Chef* finalist Kevin Gillespie, Woodfire Grill continues to wow guests on every visit. Don't be fooled by the location (the seedier part of Buckhead) or the no-frills exterior; once inside, you'll see a modern-looking dining room. The menu has a la carte options, but to truly experience Woodfire Grill, go with the 5- or 7-course tasting menu. There isn't a printed menu for these, but you'll be surprised by each course, which is part of the appeal of going this route. The plates aren't huge portions, but each course is incredibly creative, and the ingredients mix well together. If you have a group, everyone at the table must partake in the multicourse dining option. The wine list is extensive and the sommelier can give you a recommendation. At the end of the meal, get the coffee; you'll get your own French press.

Downtown

For many years, Downtown Atlanta was a mecca for businesses and conventioneers and not much else. At night it was deserted; many left for their homes in the suburbs. But in the last few years, there has been a resurgence in the popularity of in-town living. With it, there's been more condo development and, as would be expected, an upswing in restaurants populating the downtown area.

 Foodie Faves

Bottle Rocket, 180 Walker St., Atlanta, GA 30313; (404) 574-5680, (404) 574-5680; http://bottlerocketatl.com; Sushi; $$. Bottle Rocket is one of those restaurant-bars that is a neighborhood favorite. The small restaurant is full of bold colors and personality and has a crowd of regulars who are extremely loyal; it's the modern-day version of Cheers of downtown Atlanta. It's ironic that it has a neighborhood vibe, because it is situated rather close to the central downtown area, in close proximity to downtown attractions but just far enough off the beaten path that visitors wouldn't know it is there unless they seek it out. It is well worth it, as the drinks are extremely well made with high-end ingredients but at reasonable prices. The focus is mainly on sushi, with some other cooked items thrown in the mix. The tuna burger with the slightest bit of panko and quail egg is one item that should be sampled. Fresh fish and seafood used in the sushi are on display at the counter. Tip: This is a great choice to stop in if you are alone; sit at the bar and have a drink and let the bartender recommend some sushi.

Cake Hag Cake Shop, 575 Boulevard St., Atlanta, GA 30312 (678) 760-6300 www.cakehag.com. Desserts; $$. There's more than just cakes at this specialty dessert store. Find cookies, bars, and even ice cream sandwiches. This is run by mother and daughter team Maggie and Katie, who've had a lifelong love of cakes and desserts in general. They insist on high-quality flour, sugar, chocolates, fruits and even liquors. Speaking of alcohol, booze seems to be a popular ingredient in many cakes like the Mojito cake, the Banana Pudding (full of whisky), and the Red Wine Velvet cake. They also offer a variety of gluten-free and low-carb cakes as well. Slices are around $2–$3 and 9-inch cakes start at $33.

Der Biergarten, 300 Marietta St. Northwest, Atlanta, GA 30313; (404) 521-2728; www.derbiergarten.com; German; $$. As the name is Der Biergarten, try to sit out in the beer garden. They have done a great job making this *biergarten* as authentic as possible. But beware that seating is first come, first serve on the patio. As to be expected there are lots of beers to choose from; the highlight is that the pricing is surprisingly low. Start with the giant pretzel, which is large enough for 2 or 3 to share and comes with 3 spicy mustards. The Reuben rolls are another favorite. Signature dishes are the wiener schnitzel or jägerschnitzel, which both are served with spaetzle. Tip: They validate parking for 3 hours.

Dua Vietnamese, 53 Broad St. Northwest, Atlanta, GA 30303; (404) 589-8889; www.yougotpho.com; Vietnamese; $. A favorite of downtown workers and students, Dua can get extremely crowded at lunch, with a line out the door. But the staff moves quickly, and patrons can get their meals in 5 to 10 minutes. With fresh ingredients delivered each day, it is a local favorite. It is not uncommon for items to sell out, so get there before the lunch rush. The pho is certainly not to be missed, whether you choose beef or chicken. *Mi xao* (stir-fried noodles) and *com bo luc lac* (rice with shaking beef) and lemongrass tofu are other highlights. Note: Dua closes at 5 p.m., so it is not open for dinner, and it's only open Monday through Friday, so no weekends.

El Myr, 1091 Euclid Ave. Northeast, Atlanta, GA 30307; (404) 588-0250; www.elmyr.com; Mexican; $. El Myr is located in the

Little Five Points area of Atlanta. The somewhat artsy and eclectic neighborhood draws in a crowd and staff with tattoos and piercings. This is a true dive bar, but the burritos are so delicious, it becomes easy to overlook the atmosphere. Start with the guacamole and salsa as they are both extremely fresh. The margaritas are strong and tasty. The burritos are huge but reasonably priced. Interesting choices are the pad thai burrito and the tofu burrito. There are lots of vegetarian options like the potato, corn, and black olive burrito. The patio is wonderful for chilling with friends on a warm spring day. Extras: They are open late and have a jukebox with a good music selection.

Elliot Street Pub, 51 Elliott St. Southwest, Atlanta, GA 30313; (404) 523-2174; www.elliottstreet.com; Deli/Pub; $. This pub is teeny-tiny but huge on hospitality and friendliness. As is usual with the Castleberry Hill neighborhood, it definitely has a regular crowd, and they populate this bar most nights, but on weekend nights it can be especially difficult to find a spot inside. The small menu is mostly deli-style sandwiches, but they are made from scratch and extremely tasty. Roast beef and cheddar on ciabatta is a popular sandwich. For a twist on pastrami, try the Greek pastrami with feta cheese and tzatziki sauce. The beer selection is huge, especially for a small bar, and it is mostly what draws in the crowd. Since it is a tiny spot, the party often spills out onto the street.

Fox Brothers BBQ, 1238 Dekalb Ave., Atlanta, GA 30307; (404) 577-4030; www.foxbrosbbq.com; Barbecue; $$$. Arguably some of the best barbecue in the city, Fox Brothers BBQ was not open for long before it exploded in popularity. It is truly a mecca for fried foods. For starters the fried pickles and the fried ribs are

top choices. For wing lovers, the smoked wings are a must-try; the overall smoky, sweet, and citrus flavors come through and meld perfectly with the moist meat underneath the skin. The ribs and pulled pork are tremendous. So is the burger: chopped brisket, pimiento cheese, plus a couple strips of bacon. Just note that the actual barbecue goodness seems to get lost in the rest of the sandwich, but overall it is a crowd favorite. However, sides shouldn't be overlooked. Southern favorites like collard greens and black-eyed peas are done perfectly. Don't forget to try the burnt ends—i.e., the ends of the brisket smoked for an extra amount of time. Regulars love them. If you are feeling adventurous, try the Frito pie. (Tips: While there isn't much parking in the front of the building, it can easily be found on the side streets. Expect to wait on weekends and before Braves games.)

Gato Bizco, 1660 McLendon Ave. Northeast, Atlanta, GA 30307; (404) 371-0889; Breakfast/Brunch; $. Open until 3 p.m. only. Don't expect dinner here, but do expect to find yummy meals and friendly service in this small space. (Note: It may or may not be a requirement to have several tattoos to work here. If that makes you uncomfortable, then seek a meal somewhere else.) Sweet potato

pancakes are reason alone to make this
place a brunch destination. Omelettes
and huevos rancheros are the highlights
of the menu. Sit at the bar if you're by
yourself or are a party of two and prefer to
be seated immediately; otherwise be prepared for a short wait for
a table.

The Glenwood, 1263 Glenwood Ave., Atlanta, GA 30316; (404)
622-6066; www.glenwoodatlanta.com; Gastropub; $$. The Glenwood
is much more than a simple pub, as many may mistake it for. It has
a rather pretty interior with dark woods. Although the beer selec-
tion is good, the wine selection is pretty expansive as well. Get the
fried pickles and you won't be disappointed. Don't miss out on the
charcuterie or the cheese plates with items like *finocchiona* (fennel
salume) and Pecorino Gran Riserva cheese. When they have cala-
mari as an appetizer, it is fantastic, as are the entrees that include
venison stew and the trio of rabbit. There's so much more on this
menu than typical bar food. Closed Monday, the restaurant opens
Tues through Thurs at 3 p.m., and Fri through Sun at 11 a.m. Tip:
There is a lot in the back for parking.

Googie Burger, 190 Marietta St., Centennial Olympic Park,
Atlanta, GA 30342; (404) 223-GOOG; www.googieburger.com;
Burgers; $. Let's be real: The name is rather silly; however, the
food is quite good. Googie Burger is centrally located in Centennial
Olympic Park, so many like to grab their food and eat in the park

on warm days. They have burgers, chicken sandwiches, fries, and shakes. The fries are all-natural, not the frozen kind. Sandwiches here are huge and very filling. Go all out and order a milk shake: The peach is one of the tastiest on the menu. Adults will appreciate the beer, wine, and "spiked" milk shake options. Note: They use peanut oil for frying, so be careful if you have peanut allergies.

Graveyard Tavern, 1245 Glenwood Ave. Southeast, Atlanta, GA 30316; (404) 622-8686; www.graveyardtavern.com; American; $$. Located in the East Atlanta neighborhood, Graveyard Tavern is a pub with some upscale menu options. Open late (until 3 a.m.), this is a popular spot for a 20-something crowd, although older folks won't feel out of place on weeknights. There really is something for everyone here. There are darts and pool tables, and there's a downstairs where a DJ spins music. There's wing night Tuesday, and even a menu with classy options like duck breast. Other notable items are the burgers, caprese salad, and fish-and-chips. Note: Smoking is allowed inside, so if smoke bothers you, perhaps go elsewhere.

The Greek Gyros and Pizza, 209 Edgewood Ave., Atlanta, GA 30312; (404) 254-2899; www.thegreekatl.com; Greek; $. I've shared with you that **Nick's Food to Go** (p. 55) is home to one hell of a delicious gyro, but another entry into the classic gyro scene is The Greek Gyros and Pizza. This is located in the Sweet Auburn Curb Market, along with some other Downtown restaurants. The gyros are quite large, and the ingredients are completely fresh—tomatoes, feta, onions, and, of course, the meat is rotisserie roasted. The pizzas are made with white cheddar, a perfectly balanced sweet and spicy sauce, and crispy crust that all work together flawlessly. Of course, if it is traditional Greek items like gyros, hummus, and spanakopita that you crave, they have them on the menu as well. Tip: They sell pizza by the slice, and you can even get it with gyro meat on it.

Grindhouse Killer Burgers, 209 Edgewood Ave., Atlanta, GA 30303; (404) 522-3444; www.grindhouseburgers.com; Burgers; $. Grindhouse is located in the Sweet Auburn Curb Market. As the market is part of a large shopping area, seating is limited. These burgers are ground fresh and served medium, well done upon request. Guests can build their own burger or choose from the Grindhouse burgers. The Apache, which comes with Pepper Jack cheese and New Mexico chiles, is a great choice for a slightly spicy burger. The Yankee, with bacon and blue cheese, is another good choice. Don't forget the sides. Crinkle-cut french fries are a good standard, but the Vidalia onion rings with their sweet taste are a perfect accompaniment to the spicy Apache burger; the fresh-cut, spice-dusted sweet potato kettle chips are a perfect pairing with the Yankee. Lines can get really long on weekends after noon, so it is recommended to arrive early. (Note: Parking is not free in the SACM lot. Grindhouse offers validated parking for only 90 minutes.) Open only until 4 p.m. each day; closed Sunday.

Holy Taco, 1314 Glenwood Ave. Southeast, Atlanta, GA 30316; (404) 230-6177; www.holy-taco.com; Mexican; $$. Another gem in the East Atlanta village, Holy Taco fits the bill for both adventurous and not-so-adventurous eaters. Brisket, chicken-heart, and beef-tongue tacos can all be found here. Unless you're starving, two tacos are enough satisfy an appetite. Other menu highlights include the posole, *chilaquiles,* and roasted corn on the cob. The organic margaritas are highly addictive, but watch out: They can sneak up on you. The menu is seasonal and does change often. Although it is a casual spot, it is somewhat of a hybrid between American Mexican and authentic Mexican, so don't expect free chips and salsa and other traditional freebies associated with a typical Mexican restaurant and you won't be disappointed. When it gets crowded, it can be extremely noisy, but at the same it's a great people-watching spot. Tip: Wednesday nights are 2-for-1 appetizers at the bar.

Lotta Frutta, 590 Auburn Ave. Northeast, Atlanta, GA 30312; (404) 588-0857; www.lottafrutta.com; Latin; $. One of the most unusual and popular restaurants in the downtown area is Lotta Frutta; customers haven't stopped singing its praises since its opening. This is a healthy store that focuses on fresh fruit cups, smoothies, and vegetarian sandwiches. However, vegetarians and carnivores alike love it. It is the perfect fix for something substantial but not meaty or greasy. Get the Dolce Vitta fruit cup, which is fruit topped with vanilla yogurt, granola, and honey. Sandwiches are served on sweet Latin bread, which is pressed panini-style. The Just Veggin' is a highlight with Havarti cheese and fresh vegetables. All sand-wiches are served with a side of *chulpe,* an Ecuadorian-style toasted corn. During the winter don't miss out on the tasty soups. Quinoa soup is one of the tastiest. Tip: Inca Cola (a Peruvian favorite) is served here. Closes at 5 p.m.

Lunacy Black Market, 231 Mitchell St. Southwest, Atlanta, GA 30303; (404) 736-6164; www.lunacyblackmarket.com; Tapas; $$. Lunacy Black Market is brought to life by Paul Luna, the always eccentric yet dazzling chef-owner who is credited with introducing tapas to Atlanta. He inserts his name into each res-taurant he opens; others in Atlanta are Eclipse di Luna and Loca Luna, though he has no affiliation with either one today. Stepping into Lunacy, you'll feel like you've entered someone's living room rather than a restaurant. There are sofas, but there are tables as well if you prefer. Just head to an open space and settle in. Then after you get over the price shock—cost is a lot *lower* than you would expect—you'll settle in for a relaxing lunch or dinner. The menu changes often and is written on piece of cardboard—very quirky. Cabbage salad, snap beans, braised beef, and pork are wonderful and perfectly seasoned. One of the best kept secrets in the Downtown dining area, this is just right for a date or a small group of friends. They don't take reservations and groups like to linger, so arrive early for optimal seating. Tip:

Sunday includes the "chef's choice" of all-you-can-eat risotto and pasta for $9.95.

No Mas, 180 Walker St., Atlanta, GA 30313; (404) 574-5678; www .nomascantina.com; Mexican; $$. Although some of the entrees are quite good, it is the decor that is the draw to this Downtown restaurant. The two-story restaurant is outfitted in a colorful Mexican vibe. An affiliated housewares store called No Mas Hacienda is located right next door, so you can go shopping prior to or after dinner. As one might expect in this artsy neighborhood, it offers upscale Mexican furnishings. The salsa has a unique smoky flavor that is delicious. Chicken enchiladas with guajillo sauce are tasty. Since this is a large place, it is a good choice for groups. (Tip: The fourth Friday of each month is Art Stroll Friday in the Castleberry Hill neighborhood. All the galleries stay open late, and patrons can wander in and out while sipping on wine.) Note that service can be slow during these Art Stroll Fridays.

Peasant Bistro, 250 Park Ave. West, Atlanta, GA 30313; (404) 230-1724; www.peasantatl.com; American/Southern; $$$. This is upscale dining Downtown. The well-appointed restaurant overlooks Centennial Olympic Park. It is a special-occasion restaurant or a great place for a business dinner as the cuisine has something for everyone. The crab cakes are a great starter to any meal. Lamb is delicious and not gamey as it sometimes can be. The short ribs are a standout menu item. Even when full, order the Pecan Sticky Bread Pudding; even if you have only a few bites it is worth it.

Tip: All-you-can-eat mussels at the bar on Monday for $15 comes with your choice of *au nage* (garlic cream), Provençal (marinara), or curry.

The Porter Beer Bar, 1156 Euclid Ave., Atlanta, GA 31136; (404) 223-0393; www.theporterbeerbar.com; Gastropub; $$. The Porter is located in Little Five Points, that small, artsy neighborhood near Downtown. Entering the Porter, you'll be surprised how small it is, but the space is oddly laid out in that it stretches far back and wraps around to form an L-shape. Although regulars love to sit at the bar, groups gather at the many booths that line the pub. The beer menu is one of the most extensive in Atlanta. Beer pairing suggestions accompany menu items, which non–beer aficionados will appreciate. At first glance, many might dismiss this gastropub as simply a dive bar or a beer bar, not a place for eating. But they would be wrong. Dishes are inventive and high on flavor. Specials have included duck prosciutto and Vindaloo Ravioli. Regular menu items that don't disappoint are mussels and the bangers and mash potatoes. Don't forget to give the fries and hush puppies a try as well. The hush puppies with bacon and a Fuji apple dipping sauce are a nice twist on a classic Southern side. Tip: There is free parking around the back of the restaurant.

Reuben's Deli, 57 Broad St. Northwest, Atlanta, GA 30303; (404) 589-9800; www.reubensdeliatlanta.com; Sandwiches; $. Don't be

put off by the long line you'll see
when you enter Reuben's. That just
means it's good. It also moves
rather fast. If you are craving a solid
Reuben or really any New York deli-
style sandwich, this place is worth a

visit. It is a pretty authentic New York experience as the staff has a
slight attitude, but it is part of the shtick. Everything is good, but
check the specials board as they are priced lower than regular menu
items, but every bit as good. You can't go wrong with the classic
Reuben. A menu highlight is the Sera-wich with turkey, Greek mayo,
and feta cheese. So is the New Yorker with corned beef, pastrami,
and cheese. Claudio, the owner, cares about this place, gets to
know the regular customers, and is interested in turning newcomers
into regulars. Tip: They deliver or you can call ahead and your order
will be waiting for you when you arrive.

Ria's Bluebird, 421 Memorial Dr. Southeast, Atlanta, GA 30312;
(404) 521-3737; www.riasbluebird.com; Breakfast/Brunch; $. Ria's
is located directly across from an Atlanta landmark: the Oakland
Cemetery. Like **Radial** (p. 56), Ria's has somewhat of a funky atmosphere. But the food is outstanding. The *New York Times* even rated
their pancakes the best in the US. Business travelers who come to
Atlanta regularly have put Ria's on their must-visit list, slipping
away from their conferences for a taste of Ria's. Menu highlights
are the banana-walnut pancakes and the fish and grits. The grits
are cheddar-flavored and marry exquisitely with the fish. And don't

miss out on trying the biscuits and gravy. The biscuits are light and fluffy, while the gravy is rich enough to make you forget there isn't any meat in it. Brisket may seem like a strange brunch option, but it is a phenomenal dish and brisket lovers won't be let down. Other diner favorites are the breakfast burrito and the tempeh (similar to tofu) Reuben. They don't take reservations, so come prepared to wait on weekends. If you want the full experience without dealing with the long waits, visit during the week when the same menu is served.

Rolling Bones, 377 Edgewood Ave. Southeast, Atlanta, GA 30312; (404) 222-2324; www.rollingbonesbbq.com; Barbecue; $$. Rolling Bones is located in a refurbished gas station. Since it is rather small, get there before or after the lunch rush to avoid waiting for a table. It's interesting to note that they smoke their barbecue with hickory and pecan wood. The brisket and the pulled pork are the best menu options. Order a side of fries, sweet tea, and peach cobbler to complete the meal. Sweet potato lovers should give them a try as they are served up with a maple-butter sauce that is truly divine. Drive-through service is available for those who prefer to take their food to go. Note that it closes at 8 p.m. on Sun and at 9 p.m. during weekdays. No alcohol is served at the restaurant.

Rosa's Pizza, 62 Broad St. Northwest, Atlanta, GA 30303; (404) 521-2596; www.rosaspizza.net; Pizza; $. While Rosa's Pizza has expanded to a couple other locations in the metro area, nothing is quite as good as the original located in Downtown. This is probably the closest thing to New York–style pizza that can be found in Atlanta. Many Northerners proclaim it to be just as solid as the pizza joints in New York City. The pizza crust is slightly crunchy and not at all doughy. Staff is quick and efficient with a friendly demeanor. Toppings are of high quality and well distributed across the pizza. Pizza is available by the slice if you want to pop in for lunch and just want one or two slices to go. When it gets crowded, there's seating downstairs, or if the weather is cooperating, head over to Woodruff Park and enjoy eating outside.

SoBa Vietnamese, 560 Gresham Ave., Atlanta, GA 30316; (404) 627-9911; http://soba-eav.com; Vietnamese; $$$. SoBa is just off the main strip of the East Atlanta Village and is actually in a refurbished house. Residents of the EAV appreciate the proximity of a Vietnamese restaurant, which saves them the trip to Buford Highway. Jackfruit martinis are the most popular drink ordered here. Start your meal off with the steamed spring rolls; the dipping sauce that accompanies them is lick-your-plate worthy. This Vietnamese restaurant is a fantastic place to visit when in the mood for decent pho (pronounced "fa"). Pho is a noodle soup that can be made with beef, shrimp, or any number of other ingredients; the broth is clear and tasty. A plate with fresh basil, jalapeños, sprouts, and cilantro to add flavor and texture to the soup is shared with the table. If pho isn't your thing, they have lots of other tasty menu options. Noodle dishes with fish sauce are a great value. Try the grilled pork; smoky and crispy, the portion is huge. They have a full bar. Tuesday they have $3 appetizers and draft beer; on Sunday a medium bowl of pho and Bloody Mary is $10.

Social, 12 W. Peachtree Place, Atlanta, GA 30308; (404) 525-2246; socialintown.com; Mediterranean; $$$. One of the few centrally located Downtown restaurants that is truly unique and differentiates itself from the rest of the Downtown tourist traps, Social is a mix of European and North African influences, although technically classified as a Mediterranean restaurant. It is hidden away from most of the Downtown hotels, so one has to seek it out. The downstairs consists of a bar and primarily tables with barstools. For dinner, if there's a small crowd, opt for upstairs dining as the seating will be more comfortable. The combination of flavors that is evident in appetizers and entrees is sensational. Owners put lots of care and time into crafting unique and unforgettable dishes. You almost cannot go wrong with any of their appetizers. Especially tasty is the eggplant caviar, zucchini carpaccio with tapenade and orange zest, or the Andalusian meatballs with almonds and a Sherry wine sauce. For entrees try the lamb tagine or the risotto. Note: This spot is for a leisurely meal; diners in a rush should save this establishment for when they have time to spare. Tips: They have live music on the weekends.

Stone Soup Kitchen, 584 Woodward Ave., Atlanta, GA 30312; (404) 524-1222.; www.stonesoupkitchen.net; Breakfast/Brunch; $. They use real thick-cut bacon here, and the grits are phenomenal. One of the things that can be appreciated about Stone Soup Kitchen is that, while it is rather close to many other popular brunch spots in the city, the wait isn't ridiculously long. In fact, on weekends at peak times, it is rather easy to score a table. The patio is ideal for brunch dining. For breakfast try the Roadrunner Quesadilla with black beans and spicy red sauce served in a wheat tortilla. The SSK Burrito is a customer favorite with its pineapple salsa, as are the huevos rancheros. Vegans will appreciate Vegos Rancheros and the blueberry flapjacks. As the name suggests, the soup here is hearty and delicious, perfect for a cold winter day. The Cuban black bean, also vegan, is a customer favorite, but for something unique try the chicken curry soup over rice soup. Tip: Visit their website for coupons.

Truva, 60 Andrew Young International Blvd., Atlanta, GA 30303; (404) 577-8788; www.truvaatlanta.com; Mediterranean; $$$. There's a lunch buffet for $10 to get a sampling of different menu options. You can order off of a regular menu if you prefer, but wait times can be rather long at lunch. For starters the hummus, baba gha-noush, and stuffed grape leaves are all winners. This is a great spot for a business dinner for those attending a conference Downtown; visiting in the evening rather than lunchtime is recommended. At lunch the service is slower and you get a better selection at the buffet. At dinner they cater to large groups, there's belly dancing, and even later in the evening, it takes on somewhat of a clubby vibe for those of you who enjoy that.

Urban Cannibals Bodega + Bites, 477 Flat Shoals Ave. Southeast, Atlanta, GA 30316; (404) 230-9865; www.facebook .com/urbancannibals; Sandwiches; $$. Located in East Atlanta not far from downtown, Urban Cannibals is part grocery store, part deli, and part restaurant all in one. Not only do they have meats, vegetables, and other staples to cook with at home, but while you're shopping you can place an order to go, so this is great spot to pick up something to take home, too. Highly recommend is the Reuben (regular or turkey), the Cuban sandwich or the lamb gyro. It is a good spot for vegetarians, too; they even make a tofu gyro. They serve brunch and dinner in addition to lunch options. Many of the ingredients used in their sandwiches are organic. Most of the their orders are called in, so if you don't want to wait, call ahead as wait times can be long during peak hours. Tip: They also sell King of Pops ice pops, so you can pick them up here rather than having to drive to their cart.

Victory Sandwich, 280 Elizabeth St., Atlanta, GA 30307; (770) 676-7287; www.vicsandwich.com; Sandwiches; $. Soon after this sandwich shop opened up, it became one of the most popular in town. One of the nice things about the sandwiches here are that they are slider sized and slider priced. Most of the sandwiches will only run you about $4. Try the Hambo: prosciutto, mozzarella, arugula, apple, and reduced balsamic. Or try the Castro—slow-roasted pork, ham, fontina cheese, and yellow mustard—or the panini-style pressed Lamborghini with Italian meat and cheese. As they are rather small, you'll probably need to order two to get full. This is the kind of establishment where one would want to hang out, as they've got a Ping-Pong table and also play movies on the wall. Rumors are that the Jack-n-Coke slushie is quite fabulous. They are open until 2 a.m., so it is a cool late-night option.

Landmarks

Agave, 242 Boulevard Southeast, Atlanta, GA 30312; (404) 588-0006; www.agaverestaurant.com; Southwestern; $$$. The unique interior of this restaurant is reminiscent of an old Spanish church. The cuisine is upscale Southwestern if ever there was. Seafood lovers who happen to also enjoy Southwestern will especially appreciate the menu here. It might sound clichéd, but the guacamole is fantastic here and a wonderful start to a meal. The restaurant is known for its cayenne fried chicken breast, and it is one of the most pop-ular dishes on the menu along with the Spicy Tequila Añejo Shrimp. For something more Tex-Mex-like order the Southwestern Burrito & Stew—the huge burrito is packed with flavor, but the Hatch green-chile stew that accompanies it is what makes the meal. It can get very crowded, so reservations are a must. (Tips: Sit at the bar weekdays between 5 and 7 p.m. for 2-for-1 appetizer specials. And save room for dessert, as the dark chocolate ganache torte and key lime pie are not to be missed.)

Ann's Snack Bar, 1615 Memorial Dr., Atlanta, GA 30317; (404) 687-9207; Burgers; $. Long before burgers and hot dogs became hip and trendy, Ann's Snack Bar was serving them up. The trip to Ann's is as much about the experience as it is about trying the famous Ghetto Burger. An unwritten guideline is that you only enter if there are empty barstools (you can tell from the outside). There is little to no space to stand inside. It is one of those quirky rules of the owner, Ann. Choose to enter when the restaurant is full, and Ms. Ann herself may just eject you! She runs the entire place and scuttles around cooking, making lemonade, etc., so she has little time to converse with customers. You'll also have to be patient while food is prepared. Don't come here in a hurry or on a lunch hour. Having said that, the burger is well worth the wait. The burger is a monstrosity—two patties, not one. Even for those who come hungry, it is a still a feat to finish the entire thing. Cash only.

Atlanta Grill (Ritz-Carlton), 181 Peachtree St., Atlanta, GA 30303; (404) 659-0400, (404) 659-0400; www.ritzcarlton.com; American/Southern; $$$$. Worth it for a splurge or when cel-

AGATHA'S—A TASTE OF MYSTERY!

Agatha's (161 Peachtree Center Ave., Atlanta, GA 30303; 404-584-2255; www.agathas.com; American; $$$$) is the original comedy murder mystery theatre in Atlanta. Though it has had several locations, each show is entertaining and leaves guests in stitches. The actors are all very talented and keep the laughter going. There's no stage as the actors move around all tables. Part of the show's fun is that somehow the guests are all given a role in the play. It may be a small part but it keeps everyone entertained. Dinner is a 5-course meal of appetizers, soup, salad, choice of entree, and dessert, and the play is enacted between dinner courses, so interruptions are not a worry.

ebrating a special occasion, the Atlanta Grill will spoil you with its downright Southern hospitality and exquisite food. Although the decor inside is beautiful, seating outside is where all the action is. Perched several stories above the hustle and bustle of the streets of Downtown Atlanta, watch the action below as you sit nestled in your nook. The menu isn't huge, but it has some standouts. It is mostly seafood and steaks with a few Southern favorites thrown in, a nod to the old South—as one would expect from a restaurant of Ritz-Carlton caliber. Staff works together to provide an outstanding meal and experience, all the while making it seem effortless.

FAB, 30 Ivan Allen Jr. Blvd., Atlanta, GA 30308; (404) 266-1440; www.fabatlanta.com; French; $$$$. FAB, as French American Brasserie is also known, is an upscale downtown restaurant. The decor is beautiful, and service is exceptional. Probably one of the lesser-known restaurants to conventioneers and out-of-towners, it is definitely a cut above some of the other Downtown establish-ments. What it isn't, however, is cheap. This is a restaurant to visit when celebrating a special occasion or out on a business meeting. For starters get the *foie gras* or one of their soups. Even in the summer their soups are enjoyable. The white bean–truffle oil soup is a hefty portion and packs a lot of flavor, as does the creamy onion soup. Their signature dish is skate wing with brown-butter sauce. Another highlight on the menu is the duck confit: Cooked perfectly, the duck is seared crispy on the outside and juicy on the inside. There's a beautiful rooftop patio for warm nights. Tip: The dress code here is pretty dressy—not the place to walk into wearing a pair of jeans.

Gladys Knight and Ron Winans' Chicken and Waffles, 529 Peachtree St. Northeast, Atlanta, GA 30308; (404) 874-9393; www .gladysandron.net; Southern/Soul; $$. The name may imply a super-casual atmosphere, but this restaurant has dark colors and wide, comfy booths. Despite the restaurant's name, be advised that there is only one item with chicken and waffles in it—appropriately called Midnight Train; obviously this is their signature entree. It comes with a large waffle and four huge wings. The portion is more than enough for one person. Make sure to get bites of the chicken and waffle soaked in syrup. For an extra oomph, splash some hot sauce on top. Lots of Southern sides are found on the menu, like the fried green tomatoes, collards, and mac 'n' cheese. A perfect meal for two is ordering the Midnight Train and the Veggie Soul (pick any four vegetables) and sharing it all. Finish your meal with the sweet potato cheesecake, and you won't be disappointed. Note: There will be long waits for a table at peak times, and it is a favorite visit of conventioneers.

Nick's Food to Go, 240 Martin Luther King Jr. Dr. Southeast, Atlanta, GA 30312; (404) 521-2220; www.nicksfood.com; Greek; $. The bright blue and white walls may conjure up memories of the movie *My Big Fat Greek Wedding*. But don't be fooled by the exterior— Nick's serves up some of the best gyros in town. A gyro order plus Greek fries is enough to feed two. The fries are are truly unique and worth trying: fried potato wedges sprinkled with lemon juice and oregano and served with tzatziki sauce. Notable dishes, when available, are the Greek lasagna and the moussaka. Note: There are no tables inside—take-out only. Closes at 7:30 p.m. on weekdays, 7:00 p.m. on Saturday, and closed all day Sunday.

One Flew South, 6000 N. Terminal Pkwy., Atlanta, GA 30320; (404) 816-3464; www.oneflewsouthatl.com; Asian/American; $$$$. When one thinks of airport dining, "sophisticated" is not the first word that comes to mind. However, that's just what you can expect at One Flew South. Located in Terminal E of Hartsfield Airport, the restaurant has been open since 2008, surprising weary travelers with their upscale cuisine. The decor alone sets the tone with its white and wood elements and the forest painted on the walls. At the helm is Duane Nutter, who's competed on *Iron Chef*. Start with the scallops or pork belly sliders. Skip sushi in favor of entrees like the Kobe burger or the any dish with duck. The beer, wine, and cocktail list is solid as well. The staff makes excellent recommendations. Note: An 18 percent gratuity is automatically added to the bill.

Radial, 1530 Dekalb Ave., Atlanta, GA 30307; (404) 659-6594; www .radial.us; Breakfast/Brunch; $. The food at Radial is creative and fun. Think Oreo pancakes to lime-coconut vegan cakes. Don't miss out on biscuits covered in savory rosemary gravy. Smoked Gouda Scramble is a menu highlight: This huge burrito comes with pork or turkey, tomatoes, basil, and Gouda and is absolutely bursting with flavor. During weekends, more brunch options are offered, including specials like Flan-stuffed French Toast with Apricot-Mojito Sauce. There are lots of veggie and vegan options, too. Staff is friendly and accommodating about requests. If you prefer to patronize "green" restaurants, then this is one to visit. Late risers will appreciate that they serve brunch late on weekends until closing at 3:30. Plenty of parking is available.

Six Feet Under, 415 Memorial Dr., Ste. E, Atlanta, GA 30312; (404) 523-6664; www.sixfeetunderatlanta.com; Seafood; $$. The restaurant, located across the street from a cemetery, is appropriately named. When the weather is nice patrons fill the rooftop patio, which overlooks Oakland Cemetery. Want to try something a little different? How about the Rat Toes? These are jalapeño-stuffed shrimp wrapped in bacon. Fried green tomatoes and scallops and grits are Southern favorites that shouldn't be missed. The shrimp here is very tasty and fresh, whether it is fried or blackened, and the blackened catfish is delicious as well. Although the restaurant is primarily seafood-oriented, their burger is quite good and is almost a secret around Atlanta; given how plentiful the seafood selection is, most people gravitate toward that. The beer selection is also plentiful. This is a fantastic end to a tour of the historic Oakland Cemetery. They don't take reservations but do take call-ahead seating.

Sun Dial, 210 Peachtree St. Northwest, Atlanta, GA 30303; (404) 589-7506; www.sundialrestaurant.com; American; $$$$. One of the most touristy places in Atlanta is the Sun Dial, the rotating restaurant and bar that sits atop the Westin Hotel in Downtown. The views are spectacular, and when visiting it is worth sitting down and enjoying a drink while the restaurant revolves with spectacular views of the Atlanta skyline. Service is solid. The food is decent but isn't the most innovative out there. Think steaks, pasta, and fish. Lunch is a terrific choice for those wanting to experience the restaurant at about half the price. The atmosphere is perfect for a romantic evening. It is certainly a special occasion restaurant. On the floor above, you can see lots of historic memorabilia and learn interesting facts about Atlanta. (Note that this floor doesn't move.) It is definitely a place to take out-of-towners to impress them with the views of the city. Parking can be problematic; try to visit during the day for better parking and for lower prices.

Thumbs Up Diner, 573 Edgewood Ave. Northeast, Atlanta, GA 30312; (404) 223-0690; www.thumbsupdiner.com; Breakfast/ Brunch; $. Reasonable pricing and consistent food are what you'll find at Thumbs Up Diner. Menu highlights are the french toast made with challah and the Sassy Scramble, which is eggs with cream cheese. If you've never had chicken and waffles and want to give them a try, this is a good restaurant to sample them. Want a skillet breakfast that comes with everything mixed up? Try the Heap: A huge portion, it comes with home fries, eggs, and cheese,  and just about anything else you'd like to add. For picky eaters, it is nice that their breakfasts are customizable; called Build Your Own Breakfast, one could order 2 eggs with cheese and a pancake with spuds (home fries). (Tip: Don't miss out on their jams. Rather than store-bought jams, theirs are house-made.) Note that payment is cash only, but they do have an ATM on-site. Waits can be very long on weekends.

The Vortex, 438 Moreland Ave. Northeast, Atlanta, GA 30307; (404) 688-1828; www.thevortexbarandgrill.com; Burgers; $. Enter through the large skull to the main dining area of the Vortex. Once inside, choose from a selection of burgers. You may remember that they were featured on the show *Man v. Food*. You really can't go wrong with any of the choices. The bacon-and-blue-cheese burger is terrific. So is the cowboy burger with ham and barbecue sauce. But if you really want the ultimate burger (the one that was featured on *Man v. Food*), order the Coronary Bypass, a ½-pound burger with 3 slices of cheese, 4 strips of bacon, and a fried egg on top. Skip the fries and order the much better Tater Tots. There are a ton of beer choices, and they have a fully stocked bar, too. Part of the gimmick of the Vortex is that the servers here have a small attitude. It isn't rudeness, but if you are expecting a place where the servers fawn all over you, this isn't it. This is most certainly not a place to bring children. They do allow smoking here. Tip: free dinner on your birthday.

Specialty Stores & Markets

Le Petit Marché, 1963 Hosea Williams Dr., Atlanta, GA 30317; (404) 371-9888; www.thelittlemarket.net; $. Located in the growing neighborhood of Kirkwood, this specialty grocer and cafe offers a wide array of locally produced and artisan foods, as well as gift items. Owner Marche makes it a point to interact with customers and ensure everyone has a good experience. They have a nice breakfast/brunch offering that is served all day. Try the grits stack, a variation on shrimp 'n' grits. The shrimp po'boy and spicy tuna sandwiches, as well as their Chinese chicken salad and house-made soups, are standouts. They also serve breakfast all day. Open 8 a.m. to 4 p.m. daily.

The Mercantile, 1660 Dekalb Ave., Atlanta, GA 30307; (404) 378-0096; www.themercantileatl.com; Specialty Foods; $$. This specialty grocery store has only been open since 2008, but it has already become a neighborhood favorite. Expect to find a variety of herbs, spices, Asian goods, organic pastas and canned goods, and fresh produce. Although they stock high-end (read: pricey) groceries, they also carry a decent variety of wines and some tasty sandwiches. The Kirkwood is a customer favorite with thick bacon, avocado, onions, and mayo. Many of the other sandwiches are named for nearby Atlanta neighborhoods—e.g., the Druid Hills, the Candler, and the Reynoldstown. The Chicken and egg salads are also tasty, but you can find out-of-the-ordinary bites such as the black bean quinoa sliders. They offer very fresh breads as well. Bring your credit card, as the place isn't cheap, and you'll be tempted to stock up on all the unique goodies.

The Sweet Auburn Curb Market, 209 Edgewood Ave., Atlanta, GA 30303; (404) 659-1665; www.sweetauburncurbmarket.com; $$. This market is rich with history, as is evident with just a glance. It is filled with grocery items and the freshest meats and seafood available in Atlanta. Even obscure items like oxtails or frog's legs can be found here. In addition to the many vegetables, meats, and seafood for sale, small cafes line the outer edges of the market, encouraging shoppers to eat before or after they've made their purchases. These include bakeries, candy stores, a coffee shop, and African, Southern, burger, and Italian restaurants. All are small businesses that are relatively new and not able to afford to rent a space on their own yet. Several restaurants that are now thriving in Atlanta got their start at the Sweet Auburn Curb Market.

Virginia Highland/
Inman Park

The Virginia Highland part of town is an old and historic part of the city. The area comprises the Inman Park and the Old Fourth Ward. Once thought to be on the decline due to crime and moves to the suburbs, this area has seen a resurgence in the last handful of years. Some very high-end restaurants have established themselves and are really helping to anchor the neighborhood.

Foodie Faves

Babette's Cafe, 573 N. Highland Ave., Atlanta, GA; (404) 523-9121; www.babettescafe.com; French; $$$. Babette's Cafe has been on the Atlanta dining scene since the 1990s. Steeped in history, this quaint restaurant is situated in a refurbished house on the outskirts of the Virginia Highland area. The house was built in 1916. With an outdoor deck that is prime real estate during warm months, it is a short cab ride away from Downtown. Away from the trendy bars and crowded areas of the Virginia Highland neighborhood, Babette's Cafe is somewhat of a hidden gem in the area. Patrons especially like to visit during weekend for brunch as their french toast with bananas and caramel sauce is outstanding. Don't miss Babette's Punch, a unique twist on a mimosa. For dinner your best bet is to stick with the small plates. Order the gaufrette potato with warmed Gorgonzola cheese sauce, and the mussels served with strawberries and serrano peppers. Tuesday, Wednesday and Thursday nights offer a prix-fixe meal for less than $20. Babette's has a notable wine selection and won a *Restaurant Hospitality* magazine award for best short wine list. Reservations recommended. See Babette's Cafe's recipe for **Steamed Mussels with Strawberries & Serrano Peppers** on p. 224.

Cafe Circa, 464 Edgewood Ave., Atlanta, GA 30312; (404) 477-0008; www.cafecircaatl.com; Caribbean; $$. Cafe Circa is one of the true hidden gems that border Edgewood and Boulevard. Their rooftop deck is inviting and looks like a fun time for a girls' night out. The Caribbean menu has so many interesting-sounding dishes on it. For starters, choices include empanadas, curried mussels, goat stew, and conch cakes. The ackee (national fruit of Jamaica) and saltfish (cod) is a unique item and a bit of an acquired taste. For mains, you can't go wrong with the scallops or the shrimp and grits. The perfectly cooked scallops are matched with a spicy tomato emulsion and pureed sweet potatoes. Even the curried cabbage can't be left behind on your plate. Service is really friendly. Tip: Most Monday nights include the musical stylings of singer Francine Reed.

Floataway Cafe, 1123 Zonolite Rd., Ste. 15, Atlanta, GA 30306; (404) 892-1414; www.starprovisions.com; American; $$$. Part of the Star Provisions group (which also includes **Bacchanalia,** p. 102, and **Quinones at Bacchanalia,** p. 106), this is one of the less pricey restaurants in the group. The decor is minimalist and modern at Floataway. For a romantic evening, opt to sit outside in the courtyard under the stars. The menu is interesting in that there are unique items that make it a great fit for foodies, yet there are simple pizzas and pastas that will please picky eaters. The menu changes quite often, but customer favorites remain. Regulars love to get the quail, gnocchi, and trout. Don't miss the tuna *crudo* appetizer to start. Desserts are superb, and it would be a tragedy to leave without having one. The toffee cake, moist and delicious, is the perfect ending to a meal here. Note: The restaurant can be difficult to find; it is located in the back of what seems to be an industrial complex.

Fontaine's, 1026 N. Highland Ave., Atlanta, GA 30306; (404) 872-0869 http://nnnwcorp.com/fontainesmainpage.html; Seafood; $$. Fontaine's was named after Fontaine Weyman, the uncle of owner Sam Weyman. From the outside, the bright neon sign that marks Fontaine's is in stark contrast to the other Virginia Highland restaurants. Many patrons love the bar and sit and enjoy catching up with friends there or grab a meal alone. The bar spans the entire length of the restaurant and is a perfect option if you are flying solo. The lobster bisque is excellent, with large chunks of lobster and has the perfect combination of sweet and salty. Sides of Tater Tots and fried okra are highly recommended. They have complimentary valet. (Tip: Tuesday nights are half off oysters. It is very popular and gets very crowded, so try to arrive early.)

4th and Swift, 621 North Ave., Atlanta, GA 30308; (678) 904-0160; www.4thandswift.com; Modern American; $$$. This was one of the restaurants to open up at a very difficult time in 2008, when the economy was barely hanging on, so it is a testament to what a terrific place it is and the quality of food that it has remained popular and been able to sustain itself. With its stained concrete flooring, high ceilings, and low lighting, it has an overall industrial look and feel. If it is a special occasion, ask for seating in the curved booth against the wall of the restaurant. It gives a great view of the restaurant, bar area, and the kitchen. The bread basket consists of crispy flatbread and cheddar garlic rolls that tempt you to fill up on them. The Modern American menu is seasonal, so it changes frequently, as do the specials. Expect to find shredded lamb with a spicy harissa and crispy cod over couscous. They have just over 10 beers to chose from, a good mix, but you won't find the common domestics here; it is an eclectic mix from small breweries. The wine list has some wonderful options, especially if you are a fan of reds. Tip: Although the restaurant has valet service, you are free to park your car in the lot if you can find an empty space.

Fritti, 311 N. Highland Ave., Atlanta, GA 30307; (404) 880-9559; www.frittirestaurant.com; Pizza; $$. Fritti pizza is one of the few *napolitano* pizzas around. Of course, there is **Varasano's** (p. 31) in Buckhead and **Antico** (p. 100) in the Westside, but the atmosphere of Fritti is truly memorable versus these other two. Skip the appetizers and head for the main attraction: pizzas. They have a ton of pizzas to choose from, and there's a kind to suit anyone's taste. Although the standouts are the calamari pizza and the mushroom pizza, if you are a meat lover order the Maialona, Fritti's version of a meat lover's pizza. The soft yet crispy crust is done just right. The smoked mozzarella is very fresh as are all the toppings. The wine list has many options by the glass. It can get quite loud at this restaurant, so it is great for a get-together or girls' night out but not the best choice for a quiet evening of catching up. Save room for the panna cotta dessert. Don't be fooled by the fact that it is a pizza joint; make reservations or expect to wait for a table. Tip: If you take advantage of the complimentary parking across the street, don't forget to have your ticket validated inside.

Goin' Coastal, 1021 Virginia Ave., Atlanta, GA 30306; (404) 941-9117; www.goincoastalseafood.com; Seafood; $$$. One of the biggest changes in restaurants in the Atlanta area of late is the move toward sustainable farm-to-table and locally sourced foods. It is not uncommon to read on menus where the food comes from if they claim that it is indeed locally sourced. Servers proclaim the humane treatment of everything that appears on the menu. Start your meal off with the fried pickles and their daily selection of fresh oysters. The presentation is beautiful. The wine list is great for those who enjoy wine, but don't miss out the imaginative and inventive cocktails that they offer. The lobster tacos, with pieces of lobster fried in tempura batter, are light and tasty and although an entree, they make a ter-rific appetizer for 2–3 people, allowing you to save room for more substantial entrees. While there are obviously daily specials, the trout lightly fried in Goin' Coastal's special seasoning blend is per-fectly spiced and cooked just right. Meat lovers won't regret their choice either, as the pork belly is tender and juicy, too. Valet is $3 and is located across the street.

Miso Izakaya, 619 Edgewood Ave., Atlanta, GA 30312; (678) 701-0128; www.misoizakaya.com; Japanese; $$. In Japan, an *izakaya* is known as a place to sit, relax, drink, and share small plates.

Owner Guy Hong has definitely created a pretty atmosphere for just that. Glancing over the drink menu you'll see numerous creations with *sochu,* which is the Japanese version of vodka. Drinks include lychee, watermelon, and cucumber and other refreshing flavors that marry well with *sochu.* If the miso soup with crab is available, order that to start. Then move on to the steamed buns, being sure to sample both the pork belly and duck, which will perfectly whet your appetite for the star entrees to come. Sushi is fresh and well-prepared, as are dishes like tuna tartare with quail egg on top, Madras lamb, and spicy eggplant. The presentation itself is quite breathtaking, so visually appealing it is *almost* a shame to eat the food. The calming Japanese setting makes for an enjoyable meal no matter when you visit. One of the few restaurants in the area that have their own parking lot attached, there's always plenty available. Tip: They have a late night *tonkatsu ramen* menu that is served after 10 p.m.

Noche, 1000 Virginia Ave., Atlanta, GA 30306; (404) 815-9155; www.heretoserverestaurants.com; Tapas; $$. A wide variety of tapas is offered here. This place comes alive later in the evening, hence the name Noche, Spanish for "night." As such, the restaurant can quite noisy, so it's not the choice for a quiet, intimate evening but perfect for a large group of friends. While the tapas are decent, it is the location, atmosphere, and neighborhood vibe that are the draw here. However, the Trailer Park Tacos with delectable fried chicken, queso, and *carne asada* are tasty, as is the hummus. For an interesting twist on the classic Cuban sandwich, try the Torta Cubana:

pulled pork, serrano ham, pickled jalapeños, and *mojo* dressing. Note: Everyone must be present to be seated. Tip: Monday nights have $2 tacos (excludes lobster).

Original El Taco, 1186 N. Highland Ave., Atlanta, GA 30306; (404) 873-4656; www.fifthgroup.com; Mexican; $$. The Original El Taco is located a little further down from the main drag of the Virginia Highland area. Away from the busy bars and central location, it has its own parking lot, which can get crowded on busy nights. What's also different about this restaurant is that instead of it being populated by mostly 20- and 30-somethings like the other restaurants in the Virginia Highland neighborhood, there is a mix of young, old, and families. Yes, even children are present early in the evening. It is probably due to the fact the cuisine is Mexican, which tends to be a crowd pleaser. It also closes around 10 p.m. and isn't open late like some of the other restaurants in the Highlands. When you enter the restaurant, you'll be given a numbered token. Every hour, they spin a huge wheel with prizes. If your number comes up, prizes can range from the small chips and salsa to something much larger. Start things off with the Just-Crushed guacamole or the Queso Royale, which is made with chorizo, charred onion, and jalapeños for a bit of spice. Skip main courses in favor of tacos. Most of the tacos are wonderful: chicken, fish, shrimp, or carnitas, all offered with substantial meat inside.

Parish, 240 N. Highland Ave., Atlanta, GA 30307; (404) 681-4434; www.parishatl.com/home.php; Southern/Cajun; $$$. **Parish,** a restaurant housed in a historic building from the early 1900s, was originally a heavily influenced New Orleans–style restaurant but has shifted slightly to a more Southern menu. However, the beautiful decor with exposed brick has remained unchanged, and some of the customer favorites have remained on the menu. Start things off with the charcuterie plate. Although the meats change out, they are always quality, even down to the house-made pork rind. The plate is served up with house pickles and ale mustard. The mushroom and grits is another exceptional starter, which is served up with a fried egg; the mix of the runny egg, grits, and mushrooms is perfection. True Southern favorites like the Coca-Cola-braised short ribs don't disappoint. Neither does the whole roasted fish, not only a beautiful presentation but also quite delicious. The TV Dinner plate (a meat and three) is served up in the classic cafeteria tray. If feeling gluttonous, order the burger. Made with a mix of pork and beef, it is topped with pimiento cheese, bacon, and fried green tomato. Plenty of street parking is available or opt for valet. See Chef Joe Schafer's recipe for **Mushrooms & Grits** on p. 227.

Park's Edge, 913 Bermina Ave., Atlanta, GA 30307; (404) 584-7275; www.parksedgeatl.com; American; $$$. Many of the Atlanta restaurants in historic areas are located in refurbished houses. Park's Edge is no exception. As such, it is small and gets very crowded, especially during weekend brunch. Also, the restaurant is located at the very back of an alley and is incredibly easy to miss.

So be on the lookout for their sign as you are driving down North Highland. When visiting at brunch, you'll start out with large fluffy biscuits and jelly. Don't fill up, as portions are rather large here. The peaches-and-cream french toast is very tasty and filling, but if it is a true egg breakfast you crave, then order the crab Benedict with smoked salmon. Served with poached eggs and a hollandaise sauce, it will fill you up for the entire day. Bottomless mimosas, Bellinis, and Bloody Marys are only $10.

At dinner, start with the spinach and goat cheese wontons or the spicy coconut curry mussels. Not-to-miss entrees are the blue cheese–crusted steak or the scallops. Note: Wine Down Tuesday through Thursday evenings offer $5 wine glass specials and $8 small plates specials. Reservations required, especially for brunch. Tip: Free parking along the side street.

P'cheen, 701-5 Highland Ave. Northeast, Atlanta, GA 30312; (404) 529-8800; www.pcheen.com; Gastropub; $$. P'cheen is a bit of mystery in the neighborhood in that it cannot really be pegged as a bar, restaurant, or gastropub—it is a mix of all three. Although the restaurant is small and the kitchen tiny, they do crank out some pretty phenomenal dishes. The Thai mussels and fries are a perfect start to a meal and are great for sharing. The fries come with choice of three house-made dipping sauces all equally complementary to the fries. For a main meal choose the chicken curry. All cuisines are expertly cooked, as the chef is talented at preparing each country's cuisine he represents with craft, finesse, and bold flavors. (Tip: They offer a nightly option called the Just Trust Us plate. For approximately

$8 you never know what the chef will create, but it's guaranteed to knock your socks off. One favorite, for example, was a spicy pork tostada. Ingredients are always fresh and extremely tasty.)

Serpas True Food, 659 Auburn Ave., #501, Atlanta, GA 30312; (404) 688-0040; www.serpasrestaurant.com; American; $$$. The duck rolls and the calamari are a tasty start to your meal, but do keep in mind the starters here tend to be rather small. A good rule of thumb is order one starter per guest. Some of the best entrees are the stuffed chicken breast and the trout, which is perfectly pre-pared. However, the scallops in panang curry sauce are one of the most popular menu items. The spaghetti squash served up with the scallops is slightly spicy, and although the three scallops weren't huge, they ended up being very filling. Steaks like the New York strip are prepared excellently, and if you aren't a fan of brussels sprouts, give them a try here and you might just change your mind.

The creamy grits are some of the best in the city and should definitely be ordered when they are on the menu. There's a Sunday night supper deal: For $20, you get a salad, main course, sides to share, and dessert.

The Sound Table, 483 Edgewood Ave., Atlanta, GA 30312; (404) 835-2534; http://thesoundtable.com; Tapas/American; $$$. The Sound Table, located at the corner of Edgewood and Boulevard in the Old Fourth Ward area of Atlanta, comes from the same people who brought us **Top FLR** (p. 98). It can be tricky to find the Sound Table, as it's identified only by the letters "ST" painted on the wall by the door. The cocktail menu here is very elaborate: It almost seems to be more of a focus than the food. Sample drinks include the Stone Mountain—made with cognac, pine liqueur, pear liqueur, and baked apple bitters—or the September Gurl—made with Gemini Jams fig jam, pisco, lemon, and sage. For starters, order the curried chickpeas and the *arancini* (fried rice balls coated with breadcrumbs). *Arancini* were scrumptious filled with black truffle, roasted garlic, and pecorino. The burger is quite tasty and juicy. No lettuce, tomatoes, or ketchup necessary. Go ahead and splurge on the crispy, tasty fries, too. The Chinese short ribs are also a good option if you are looking for more of a meal; the sweet chili sauce is a nice contrast to the slightly salty soy sauce and scallions.

Super Pan Latino, 1057 Blue Ridge Ave., Atlanta, GA 30306; (404) 477-0379; http://superpanlatinosandwichshop.com; Latin; $$. A creation of Chef Hector Santiago, owner of **Pura Vida** (p. 76), this is a great stop to grab a sandwich if you are in for a fix of Chef Santiago's cooking but don't have time for a lengthy meal. Located around the corner from Pura Vida, it can be tricky to find. Look for the SUPER PAN sign around the side of the Pura Vida building. Walk up the stairs and order at the counter. You can then take your food to go or take a number and they'll bring your order after you take a seat downstairs. The pork bun and the Cuban are sandwiches to try: melt-in-your-mouth pork belly with slaw on a coconut bun was a perfect pairing; the Cuban—or Media Dia, as it is called—is also quite delicious. Served up on sweet pineapple bread, the Media Dia is authentic and very fresh tasting. Finish your meal with a chocolate chip–chipotle cookie, the spiciness enhancing the chocolate in the cookie. Tip: While many take the sandwiches and go, to do the sandwiches justice eat them there if you can. While the ingredients are high quality and tasty, be prepared for some hefty prices for sandwiches.

Zuma Sushi, 701 Highland Ave., Atlanta, GA 30312; (404) 522-2872; www.zumasushibar.com; Sushi; $$$. The decor of Zuma Sushi is sleek and modern. The colors used are mostly red and black, even down to the servers' black and red kimono-like attire. Although groups of friends frequent the establishment, the smallish restaurant is mostly set up for couples. Note that the staff here is small, so service, while friendly, can be slow at times. The tuna *tataki* is excellent and the Zuma Roll and the Viagra Roll, an avocado/cream cheese roll topped with four different-colored roe, are menu highlights. Parking can be difficult to find. There is a patio for outdoor seating when weather allows. Tip: Lunch offers all you can eat for $15.

La Tavola, 992 Virginia Ave., Atlanta, GA 30306; (404) 873-5430; www.fifthgroup.com; Italian; $$$. One of the staples of any neighborhood is a solid Italian restaurant, and La Tavola definitely fits the bill. The small dining room can get loud, especially given the open kitchen, so opt for patio dining, which is open year-round. The wine list is excellent and lengthy. So skip the pricey cocktails and go straight for wine. Start with the beet and orange salad; the pistachios and red wine vinaigrette are delicious in this salad. Dishes are highly creative, like the rabbit sausage–stuffed pasta covered in swiss chard and béchamel sauce. Although dinners are phenomenal here, don't overlook brunch. Try the challah french toast with berries and honey mascarpone: The perfectly done french toast marries perfectly with the sweet mascarpone and the tart berries. Many of the other brunch items are served up with poached eggs and house-made polenta, which is a nice departure from the more traditional hash browns. For dessert, order the flourless chocolate cake that is made with olive oil. Although it sounds strange, it is quite tasty and not overly sweet for those who appreciate those kinds of desserts. Reservations necessary for weekend dining. Tip: Not feeling that hungry? Pasta entrees are available in appetizer portions for $5 less than the entree portion.

Murphy's, 997 Virginia Ave., Atlanta, GA 30306; (404) 872-0904; www.murphys-atlanta-restaurant.com; Southern; $$$. One of the most popular brunch restaurants in the city, the wait can be hours long as diners line up outside for some delicious breakfast favorites. Eggs and omelettes are great but for a Southwestern fix give the *chilaquiles* a try (shredded chicken over tortillas, fried egg, tomatillo sauce, avocado, sour cream). At dinner the lights go down and dinner service turns cozy. Although the atmosphere is slightly upscale and classy, the food is 100 percent comfort food. The spinach and sausage meat loaf is perfectly cooked. The shrimp and grits are consistently one of guests' favorite items on the menu. Skip the truffled mac 'n' cheese in favor of other sides. Tip: Drop a dollar off in the honor jar and get a huge cookie.

Pura Vida, 656 N. Highland Ave., Atlanta, GA 30306; (404) 870-9797; www.puravidatapas.com; Latin/Tapas; $$$. You may remember Chef Hector Santiago from his short stint on *Top Chef*. His talent is evident to anyone who visits his Virginia Highland restaurant. Pura Vida means "pure life" or "life is great," and the food here is some of the best Atlanta has to offer: fresh and flavorful with interesting pairings of ingredients. Think mahimahi and chorizo skewers with banana mustard. Or how about this—hearts of palm coated in coconut vinaigrette with dates, serrano ham, and tres leches yogurt. The flavors are bold and unexpected but always work well together. For starters, begin with the malanga-root chips with creamy sauce as well as the shrimp cocktail. Pork fans will love the light and fluffy steamed buns that pair well with the pork belly inside. For those feeling adventurous, order the goat *mofongo*. It is not always listed on the menu, but regulars know to ask for it. Tip: A perfect choice for a late-night dinner date after taking in an Imax movie on Friday night. They also host monthly cooking classes, where you can learn to cook the Latin dishes found on the tapas menu.

Rathbun's, 112 Krog St., Ste. R, Atlanta, GA 30307; (404) 524-8280; www.rathbunsrestaurant.com; Modern American; $$$$. Rathbun's is one of the most popular Atlanta restaurants. The chic decor with concrete floors, brick walls, and tall ceiling with exposed ductwork is very appealing. Rathbun's is as much about the food as it is about the famous chef, Kevin Rathbun. Staff is helpful and very friendly, not to mention extremely knowledge-able about the menu. They'll recommend a perfect wine pairing to complement anything ordered. The menu is divided into Small Plates, Big Plates, and Second Mortgage Plates. For small plates, the eggplant fries are huge and covered with confectioners' sugar; when dipped in the side of Tabasco, the odd combination of sweet and spicy works well for this dish. Other small plates to try are the tuna tartare and bone marrow. For sharing, the prosciutto flatbread is a perfect choice, covered in a creamy sauce and drizzled with pink peppercorn honey. The whole roasted bronzini (fish) that was served with brussels sprouts is a fish lover's dream. Crispy duck breast with Thai risotto and green curry essence is slightly spicy; heat lovers will enjoy this dish, and it is quite filling as the duck breast is quite large. Another menu standout is the smoked brisket in aged sherry-vinegar barbecue. Of course, you may remember they were featured on the Food Network's *The Best Thing I Ever Ate* for their lamb chops. It can get rather loud in the restaurant. Note: The restaurant is closed on Sunday.

Surin, 810 N. Highland Ave., Atlanta, GA 30306; (404) 892-7789; www.surinofthailand.com; Thai; $$. One of the first Thai restaurants in Atlanta, Surin remains quite popular. The seating is quite close together, and it can get noisy on weekend nights when it is filled to capacity, so not a good option for a quiet evening. They have some of the best coconut soup in the city. For entrees the barbecue chicken at lunch is terrific. For dinner don't miss out on the three-flavored fish. For soft-shell crab fans, get the flash-fried soft-shell crab with green curry sauce. Vegetarians will appreciate the tofu dishes; coconut soup and curry are both winners. Even a basic dish like pad thai is stellar here. Tip: Staff is quick to get you in and out at lunch. Even if you have a large group, they will split up the check quickly.

Two Urban Licks, 820 Ralph McGill Blvd., Atlanta, GA 30306; (404) 522-4622; http://twourbanlicks.com; Modern American; $$$. Two Urban Licks is part of the Concentrics Restaurant Group. It is probably the best and most popular of all in the group. The name just seems to exude sex appeal. Venturing to the restaurant may be a little awkward as it is in a converted warehouse. You'll enter through what seems like an updated dock door. But once inside, the sexy, chic atmosphere creates a fun time whether there for a celebration with friends or a romantic evening for two. Servers are extremely knowledgeable about both the menu and the wine and make excellent wine and food pairings. Don't miss starting the meal off with one of the house-made concoctions. The smoked salmon with chipotle cream cheese and tuna tartare are not only a great start to the meal but a beautiful presentation. For entrees order the skirt steak or scallops and grits. Tip: A secret late-night menu is available after 10 p.m. on weekends. See Chef Cameron Thompson's recipe for **Crab Beignets** on p. 229.

Wisteria, 471 N. Highland Ave., Atlanta, GA 30307; (404) 525-3363; www.wisteria-atlanta.com; American/Southern; $$$. Wisteria can be described as upscale Southern. Housed in a freestanding building with exposed brick and dark lighting, it is extremely romantic but also a fantastic choice to take an out-of-town guest. The Patrice, a signature drink made with tequila and champagne, is the perfect start to a relaxing evening. The wine list is huge. Let Katie, the general manager, pick one for you as she expertly pairs wine with your food choices. The black-eyed pea hummus served up with homemade sweet potato chips has just the right amount of garlic and lemon juice. The scallops are another hit in the appetizer department: They're a twist on bacon-wrapped scallops that use pork belly instead. The garlicky mussels and tomatoes make a great pair. By far the most popular dish on the menu is the molasses-rubbed pork tenderloin, and if you are open to it, get it done medium as the chef recommends, and you'll appreciate it. See Chef Jason Hill's recipe for **Macaroni and Cheese** on p. 230.

Specialty Stores & Markets

Belly General Store, 772 North Highland Avenue, Atlanta, GA 30306; (404) 872-1003; www.bellystore.com; Bakery/Grocer; $. Belly is steeped in history. Built in 1914, one of the most popular soda fountains, it was a gathering place for locals. It offers a combination of fresh foods like bagels and cupcakes and gift items. Belly prides itself on offering quality good and stands by the fact that nothing carried in the store is mass-produced. Bagels are standouts here. Beacuse they are cooked with olive oil, the bagels are light and chewy. Their sea salt bagels are a customer favorite. At lunch various sandwiches and paninis are offered. The only seating available is at long communal tables.

Midtown

Midtown Atlanta is home to some of the finest restaurants in the city. While the heart of Midtown has been thriving for years now, there always seem to be events geared toward bringing people into the area. These include free movies on a big screen during the summer, the "winter wonderland" that takes place in Atlantic Station during Christmastime, and Street Food Thursday, when the streets are filled with different food trucks during lunch hours and Midtown workers line up to try their treats. So while the restaurants and stores may sometimes change, Midtown keeps residents and visitors entertained with fun things in and around the area.

Foodie Faves

Abattoir, 1170 Howell Mill Rd., Atlanta, GA 30318; (404) 892-3335; www.starprovisions.com; French; $$$. The translation of Abattoir is "slaughterhouse." There couldn't be a more appropriate name for this Midtown restaurant. Not only is it located in a former slaughterhouse, but the restaurant specializes in using all parts of the animal, meaning they offer offal. Think tripe stew or lamb liver fritters. Passing by the sign featuring butcher knives, you'll enter the well-appointed space that resembles a modernized farmhouse. There's lots of action at the bar, which sits front and center, but tables are arranged for a more intimate dining experience. Outside seating is appealing, but be warned that the noisy train that comes by sporadically could interrupt your meal. It is part of the Star Provisions restaurant group, which owns **Bacchanalia** (p. 102), one of the highest rated restaurants in Atlanta. Start with the "food in a jar"—the rabbit rillettes are perfectly seasoned and spreadable. Star Provisions does a great job with cured meats, so if you are a fan of them, try the beef jerky or charcuterie plate, and you won't be disappointed. If you are a burger fiend, try the house burger, which is unlike any burger you'd find elsewhere. It is 80 percent beef and 20 percent pork, but the pork flavor shines through. Fish and scallop dishes are always prepared well with a beautiful presentation.

Apache Cafe, 64 3rd St., Atlanta, GA 30308; (404) 876-5436; www.apachecafe.info; American; $$. Apache Cafe has held a variety of arts-related events including poetry readings, some live shows, and art shows. If you need to escape the live performance, there is a back patio that serves as a secret garden, with fresh air. It can get extremely packed with popular performances, so your best bet is to call ahead and reserve a table. Note: If you park in the back make sure you pay, or your car will be towed. The jerk wings, shrimp and grits, and shrimp or spinach quesadillas are very tasty. Save room for dessert—sopapillas, brown-sugared plantains, or pear cobbler.

Apres Diem, 931 Monroe Dr. Northeast, Ste. C103, Atlanta, GA 30308; (404) 872-3333; www.apresdiem.com; European/American; $$$. Located in the Midtown Promenade Center near Piedmont Park, the restaurant is famous for coffee and desserts, but most Atlantans are unaware of the tasty and creative dinner items available. The dark and cozy atmosphere is reminiscent of cafes and bistros in Europe. The inviting couches and free Wi-Fi invite guests to hang out and drink some of their coffees. An added bonus is that there is free parking in the shopping center, a rarity in Midtown. Although they list hummus and baba ghanoush separately on the menu, ask for the combo (half of each), and servers are happy to accommodate. They contain a kick you won't find elsewhere. Also, crustacean lovers shouldn't miss the lobster crostini: Chock-full of lobster meat with spinach, mushrooms, and shallots, it is mixed with a vodka butter sauce, and it is especially sexy for couples to share. Move on to the dried fruit salad that contains cranberries, banana chips, almonds, coconut, and feta, served with honey-apple vinaigrette, it is an extremely tasty way to meet your fruit-and-vegetable quota. The most popular menu item, however, is the salmon farfalle, served in a Sambuca-thyme cream sauce; it keeps customers coming back. The wine list is well thought-out, and servers can help select the perfect wine to accompany dinner. Open late night, to 2 a.m. on weekends and midnight all other nights. Come back for coffee and dessert after slipping next door to see a flick. Mussels cooked up with beer are half-off on Monday. Tip: Sunday through Thursday they offer dinner and movie for $25 per person, which includes an appetizer, entree, and a glass of beer or wine.

Babs, 814 Juniper St., Atlanta, GA 30308; (404) 541-0888; www .babsmidtown.com; Breakfast; $$. The decor is pleasant and the atmosphere relaxed in this small and intimate restaurant. It is hidden in the basement of a brick building. Many residents aren't aware of it, so it's certainly a good choice when other more-popular brunch spots have hour-plus wait times. Waitstaff is super friendly, and many offer comic relief. Get the Crunch Omelette with hash browns mixed in or the Crab Omelette with lots of fresh crabmeat and mozzarella. Paninis are also quite good, like the chicken and brie, as are the sweet potato fries served with a spicy curried dipping sauce. Not suggested for large groups. Tip: Free parking in the attached lot.

Baraonda, 710 Peachtree St., Atlanta, GA 30308; (404) 879-9962; www.baraondaatlanta.com; Italian; $$. Baraonda puts an American spin on a diverse array of predominantly Northern Italian dishes. Pizza is the star here, served up on a thin, crispy crust. Try the *capricciosa* with mozzarella, ham, mushrooms, artichokes, and olives, or the prosciutto di Parma pizza. It is located in relatively close proximity to the Fox Theatre, so it lends itself to pretheater dining. However, note that the restaurant only accepts reservations for parties of 6 or more. They are open for both lunch and dinner.

Bocado, 887 Howell Mill Road, Atlanta, GA 30318; (404) 815-1399; www.bocadoatlanta.com; American; $$$. The minimalist design fits right in the trendy, up-and-coming Westside neighborhood. Although Bocado is open for both lunch and dinner, visit at lunch for the fabulous and unusual sandwich options (think short rib with gruyère), and leave with your wallet a little fuller. The burger with double patties, house-made pickles, and cheese is simple, light, and one of the best to be had in the city. Even non-vegetarians will love the roasted cauliflower and eggplant sandwich. The tuna BLT is another sandwich winner. There's a lovely patio, absolutely perfect when the weather allows. Tip: Parking is located in a lot just a bit up the street from the actual restaurant if street parking is hard to find.

Bone Garden Cantina, 1425 Ellsworth Industrial Blvd., Ste. 6, Atlanta, GA 30318; (404) 418-9072; www.bonegardencantina .com; Mexican; $$. Owned by the same individuals as **the Vortex** (p. 58), Bone Garden Cantina is a small restaurant tucked away in the West Midtown area. You certainly wouldn't stumble upon it, as it is located in a more industrial area of town, but it's worth seeking out. As you enter the complex make sure you drive around back, where the entrance to Bone Garden is located. The space is rather small, but they took great care to decorate in the fashion of the Dia de los Muertos (Day of Dead); that is, there are lots of skeletons painted on the wall. Start your meal off with an order of the very fresh seviche and the beet salad with oranges and queso fresco topped with a vinaigrette dressing. Everything is a la carte here—tacos, enchiladas, burritos—making it possible to try many different things. Menu highlights are the fish taco, shrimp enchilada, tamales, and *pambazo torta* (a Mexican sandwich consisting of Mexican *telera* bread tossed in adobo sauce, grilled, and stuffed with a mix of chorizo, potatoes, chipotle pepper, and onion, and topped with sour cream, lettuce, avocado, and Chihuahua cheese). Margaritas are tasty, so get a pitcher if you are with a group.

Carolyn's Gourmet, 1151 W. Peachtree St., Atlanta, GA 30309; (404) 607-8100; www.carolynsgourmetcafe.com; Sandwiches; $. There is a great ambience here with the exposed brick walls. Sandwiches have quirky names like Motivation (hot turkey and swiss with cole slaw and Thousand Island dressing on pumpernickel) to

Commitment to Excellence (a BLT with blue cheese), or the High Energy (delicious tuna melt with just a tad of mayo). With fun names like these, you can't help but feel good about your choice. You can also find quesadillas, burgers, salads, pizzas, and wraps. It isn't only the food that impressive. The

DINNER WITH THE BARD
AT THE SHAKESPEARE TAVERN

Shakespeare Tavern (499 Peachtree St. Northeast, Atlanta, GA 30308; 404-874-5299; www.shakespearetavern.com; British; $). Mostly Shakespearean plays are performed here with a few exceptions. The actors are fabulously entertaining. Note that these aren't simply plays—the entire atmosphere from the interior design to the menu completes the mood. (The menu is that of an authentic modern pub.) There's the shepherd's pie or the King's Supper Sandwich, pork loin that is stuffed with apricots and prunes and served on a baguette. The Tavern's most popular menu item is the Cornish pasty—similar to the shepherd's pie in that it has the ground beef and potatoes, but this comes in a baked crust. At intermission treat yourself to a hot apple crisp with ice cream.

service is also something to brag about. The staff is friendly and the food comes out quickly. There are great deals to be found, including a free pizza bar on Friday between 5 and 6:30 p.m. with a drink purchase from the bar. Thursday nights include a taco bar: free tacos with drink purchase. Tip: If you are a South Carolina Gamecock, this is the spot for you to get your game on. Rumor: They will give you a 10 percent discount on your meal if you show your AAA card.

Cypress Street Pint & Plate, 817 W. Peachtree St., Ste. E125, Atlanta, GA 30308; (404) 815-9243; www.cypressbar.com; Pub/Bar food; $$. Cypress Street is a welcome addition to the Midtown neighborhood that it occupies. There was a need for a bar within walking distance to the many condos and apartments in the area. There are dark woods around the bar and booths, and surprisingly the crowd doesn't seem to all be the young 20-somethings that patronize the nearby clubs. Perhaps it is because Cypress Street has a much more sophisticated beer menu than simply a few domestics. They offer several unique beer choices that change weekly. The 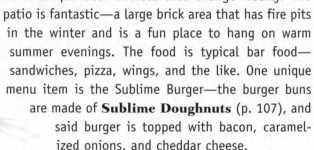 patio is fantastic—a large brick area that has fire pits in the winter and is a fun place to hang on warm summer evenings. The food is typical bar food—sandwiches, pizza, wings, and the like. One unique menu item is the Sublime Burger—the burger buns are made of **Sublime Doughnuts** (p. 107), and said burger is topped with bacon, caramelized onions, and cheddar cheese.

Deckard's, 650 Ponce De Leon Ave., Atlanta, GA 30308; (404) 941-3520; www.kitchenandkegs.com; Pub; $$$. Deckard's is upscale pub food with lots of dark wood and brick walls. There are tons of beers to choose from, and a fair handful on tap. Also, the taps change out regularly, so beer lovers are always in for something new. This doesn't mean, however, that they don't do cocktails well. Try the Moscow Mule—it packs quite a punch. For starters, try the Scotch egg with house-made sausage and beer mustard. The burgers are solid. Give the Pig Pen chorizo burger a try. It is chorizo and beef with jalapeño-cilantro relish and queso fresco. Their onion rings are huge and quite tasty as well, but mac 'n' cheese doesn't disappoint, either. For a healthier side, choose the zucchini. Fish-and-chips is served up with flounder instead of the usual cod for a twist. Service is very attentive and friendly.

Ecco, 40 7th St. Northeast, Atlanta, GA 30308; (404) 347-9555; www.ecco-atlanta.com; Mediterranean; $$$. Located in the heart of Midtown, Ecco is Mediterranean food with an excellent wine list and cocktails. One of their specialty cocktails, In the Middle of My Buchtel, is perfect for sipping on a warm summer evening. It's made from aged rum, plum puree, and purple basil, akin to a fancy mojito. And the Long Live the Queen, made with Bombay Sapphire gin, was equally tasty but a little stronger. There is a nice complexity of flavors to everything on the menu. Starters of shrimp with fennel and saffron meatballs did not disappoint. Don't be fooled by the small portions of the appetizers; they are very filling. For entrees, you can't go wrong with the fish, as they are all executed perfectly. Pastas taste like they are house-made, and the wood-fired pizzas are creative and come with quality toppings: Think sausage, Grana Padano, and house-made mozzarella. You'll want to save room for dessert with items like tangerine and hazelnut cake.

Empire State South, 999 Peachtree St., Atlanta, GA 30309; (404) 541-1105; www.empirestatesouth.com; American; $$$$. Chef-Owner Hugh Acheson and Executive Chef Ryan Smith wow guests with this relatively new restaurant that focuses on locally sourced Southern cuisine. Of course typical Southern dishes like shrimp and grits are on the menu. There's also the side of collards with ham hock. But the inventive menu pairs new and different ingredients with old favorites, like the Kimchi Rice Grits. Brussels sprouts are served shredded. While the dinner service is solid, the restaurant does its best at lunch. The trout with bacon vinaigrette is probably one of the best dishes on the menu. There's also a dish called the Super Food, which offers a sampling of five different items: hanger steak, a small salad, and various in-season vegetables. At this restaurant, you will like your vegetables, even if you've never been one to enjoy them before. At dinner, the cheese selection focuses on unique and hard-to-find cheese, and fish entrees are the best. Empire State South serves breakfast, lunch, and dinner Monday through Friday and serves brunch and dinner on weekends. Hidden at the bottom of the 999 Peachtree office building at the corner of Peachtree and 10th Street, the restaurant can be tricky to find, so be on the lookout. Oh, and if you want to get your bocce ball on, they have a bocce ball court, too. Tip: They validate parking for 3 hours in the nearby parking garage.

Flip Burger, 1587 Howell Mill Rd., Atlanta, GA 30318; (404) 352-3547; www.flipburgerboutique.com; Burgers; $$. Opened during the height of the burger craze, Flip Burger is the creation of *Top Chef* Richard Blais. It has been reviewed on CNN and in *Food & Wine* magazine, *USA Today,* and the *Wall Street Journal,* so many foodies and non-foodies seek it out based on all the exposure. The modern and trendy decor complements the innovative menu. The flat-screen televisions in framed artwork are a nice touch. Burgers range from the regular grass-fed beef burger to the steak tartare, pork chorizo, lamb, and other types that rotate out. Burger size is somewhere between a slider and regular-size burger. Skip fries in favor of the tempura-fried okra or the vodka-battered onion rings. Milk shakes like the Krispy Kreme and Nutella are tasty, and adventurous eaters will want to try the *foie gras* milk shake. Beer and specialty drinks are also served. Reservations not accepted. Expect lengthy waits during peak hours.

Fresh to Order, 860 Peachtree St. Northeast, Atlanta, GA 30308; (404) 593-2333; www.fresh2order.com; Sandwiches; $$. As the name implies, food is cooked to order. You order and pay at the counter and take your number with you and display on it on your table. When it is cold outside, the corn chowder or wild mushroom soup is warm and soothing. Best bet is to order the half-salad–half-soup combo. As for the sandwiches, the meatless sandwiches may be even tastier than the meat-centric ones. The tomato mozzarella with fresh mozzarella, roasted peppers, and basil is wonderful, as is the vegetable with grilled zucchini, avocado, squash, and feta cheese. In the salad department order the Asian salad topped with ahi tuna. Go again and again, as the menu changes often. Tip: If you are into Foursquare, the social media app, be sure to check in as Fresh to Order offers lots of great specials. There is also 1-hour free parking in the garage behind the restaurant.

Hankook Taqueria, 1341 Collier Rd., Atlanta, GA 30318; (404) 352-8881; www.hankooktaqueria.com; Korean Tacos; $. Grabbing a hold of the Korean taco craze, Hankook has garnered quite the following since opening. They were even among the first in the city to get a license to operate a food truck. There's also no table service at Hankook. Order at the counter, and your name is called when your order is ready, which is fairly quickly. The staff is extremely friendly, and the lack of table service helps to keep prices low. The smallish restaurant, located in the industrialized area of Midtown, can get very busy when the lunch crowd strikes, so try to visit at off-peak times. The menu is pretty simple at Hankook. Choices are tacos, burritos (standard chicken, beef, pork, fish, tofu, shrimp), and what they like to call "street snacks," which are really what most would consider appetizers: spicy pork sliders, tempura-fried sweet potatoes, fried dumplings, and a firedog—spicy hot dog with kimchee. Quite often the special of the day is the calamari taco, one of the best tacos there and not to be missed.

La Pietra Cucina, 1545 Peachtree St., Ste. 101, Atlanta, GA 30309; (404) 888-8709; www.lapietracucina.com; Italian; $$$$. Executive Chef Bruce Logue worked throughout Italy and the United States, including at Mario Batali's famed Babbo in New York

City, and returned to his home in Atlanta after gaining much experience and opened up La Pietra Cucina. With extensive time spent in Italy learning the cooking methods, he has mastered cooking Italian food. The menu is divided into four distinct areas: to Share, Antipasti, Primi, and Secondi. The signature entree served at La Pietra Cucina is Mario's black spaghetti with shrimp, scallions, and hot calabrese sausage, just like at Babbo. Although the menu is not huge, they have numerous nightly specials that sometimes include pasta with truffles, and these are not to be missed. Be prepared: There is lots of bold flavor in these dishes, however, the portions may not be as large as many are used to getting at traditional Italian restaurants.

Livingston, 659 Peachtree St., Atlanta, GA 30308; (404) 897-5000; www.livingstonatlanta.com; American; $$$. Livingston is an ultrachic and well-appointed restaurant and bar located across the street from the famous Fox Theatre. The design is history meets modern and trendy; it is very glamorous inside from top to bottom. Start your meal off with the tuna *crudo*. The pistachio and candied mustard play off of each other well in this starter. Short ribs are easily one of the best menu items; they nearly melt in your mouth. However, the duck breast is a close second. Tip: They have a deal on Monday called Millionaire Mondays: a lobster tail or 8-ounce filet with choice of soup or salad for $18. Another deal is a 3-course theatre menu for just under $30. Don't forget to get your parking validated. See Livingston's recipe for **Braised Short Ribs** on p. 225.

Miller Union, 999 Brady Ave., Atlanta, GA 30318; (678) 733-8550; www.millerunion.com; Southern; $$$$. One of the most talked-about restaurants since opening is easily Miller Union. The restaurant occupies the old space of the Miller Union Stockyards, hence the name. The menu focuses on farm-to-table dining; however, some of the more popular items never seem to leave the menu. When settling in, order the Miller Thyme (gin, lemonade, and thyme). The drinks are well-crafted here and use high-end liquor. Charcuterie plates don't disappoint with options like pastrami beef tongue, duck prosciutto, and duck liver terrine; they are unique and definitely a good fit for foodies. Another good starter is the Feta Snack, a spreadable feta served with vegetables. The flounder is one of the best menu items whether it is ordered at lunch in a sandwich or as a dinner entree. Short ribs and rabbit are also menu highlights.

Pasta da Pulcinella, 1123 Peachtree Walk, Atlanta, GA 30309; (404) 876-1114; http://pastadapulcinella.com; Italian; $$$. Located in a converted house, like many of the restaurants that line the side streets of Midtown, the atmosphere is charming, quaint, and heavy on romance. The view of the nearby skyscrapers is impressive. It is a perfect place to celebrate a birthday or anniversary with that special someone. The bar mixes up fantastic cocktails; however, the wine list is quite large and worth sampling a couple glasses. There are several vegetarian entrees on the menu, so it's a good choice for those who don't eat meat. The Ravioli Sardi Di Melanzane is a vegetarian entree meat lovers will love. With eggplant, bell peppers, walnuts, ricotta, Parmesan, basil, and mint, it packs in a lot a flavor. Probably the most popular item is the Tortelli di Mele, ravioli filled with browned Granny Smith apples, sausage, and Parmesan. The combination of sweet apples and salty sausage is a winning taste. There are also daily specials, of which the gnocchi and risotto are usually standouts. Think gnocchi with salmon cubes tossed in a spinach ricotta cream. The house is relatively small, so reservations are a must, especially on weekends. Note that there isn't free parking, but several lots are nearby.

Quattro, 1071 Piedmont Rd., Atlanta, GA 30309; (404) 881-0000; Italian/Pizza; $$. Quattro has a beautiful patio that is inviting on warm days; in fact it is ideal for people watching as it overlooks Piedmont Park. Pizzas and panini are the highlight here, and they serve Neapolitan-style thin crust pizzas. The hummus and bruschetta are both appetizers worth trying. For pizza, try the wild mushroom, which comes with a roasted garlic sauce, fried capers, and truffle oil in addition to mushrooms. Try the Capri sandwich, which comes with tomatoes, arugula, and chicken. They serve dinner late on weekends—open until midnight. Tip: Guests are known to let their dogs hang around the patio, so if that may be bothersome, beware.

Sausalito West Coast, 1389 Peachtree St., Atlanta, GA 30309; (404) 875-5005; Mexican; $. This Mexican restaurant is only open Mon through Fri for lunch from 11 a.m. to 3 p.m. Officially it calls itself a mix of Mexican and Chilean. Nearby office workers know that this place has great food, and it gets very crowded at peak times. Although it is not overly fancy, they do have quality food. Their steak tacos are highly recommended. The lightly seasoned steak is cut only when orders for tacos or burritos are placed, not presliced like a fast-food joint. It comes with rice and beans as well as chips and salsa all for under $10. Don't do beef? Order the sunset tacos with mahimahi. Salads come with a unique blackberry-habañero dressing, giving them a nice kick. Tip: Only a short walk from the High Museum or Colony Square area.

Spoon, 768 Marietta St., Ste. A, Atlanta, GA 30318; (404) 522-5655; www.spoonatlanta.com; Thai; $$. This small restaurant serves a bustling lunch crowd. The very tasty food at reasonable prices (lunches are only around 8 bucks) mean a wait for a table on weekdays. So be prepared that this isn't the spot to hit up if you've got to stick to an hour lunch. The portions are rather large, and you could easily make two meals out of lunches. Don't miss the scallop special when it is offered: an appetizer of 7 scallops, perfectly prepared with a slight kick—but not too hot and spicy. Another starter special is the pan-fried puff pastry. Served up with a creamy Massaman dipping sauce, it is perfect for sharing. Green curry is a menu highlight and definitely made for those who love the hot and spicy dishes. At dinner, opt for the house special—New Zealand rack of lamb with a basil sauce. Tip: There is free parking in the lot next door to the restaurant.

Tamarind Seed, 1175 Peachtree St. Northwest, Ste. 110, Atlanta, GA 30309; (404) 873-4888; www.tamarindseed.com; Thai; $$$. Tamarind is the less-expensive version of its sister restaurant **Nan Thai Fine Dining** (p. 104). From the *tuk-tuk* outside to the beautiful Thai decor inside to the waitstaff dressed in traditional attire, you'll feel welcome from the moment you enter. For appetizers, skip the more common rolls and splurge on the green papaya salad. The ever-popular pad thai is perfectly done here (not overly sweet) and well worth ordering. Standout dishes are the green curry, *kai pad prik kingh*. For a beautiful presentation order the Siam chicken, which comes served in half a pineapple. The restaurant has 4 pepper levels to choose from, so start with level 2 and, perhaps on a second visit, work your way up to level 3. Get a Thai iced tea or coffee during or after your meal, for a refreshing, slightly sweet pick-me-up. The restaurant has a Midtown location, convenient especially if staying at the W Hotel in Midtown, as this restaurant is a short walk from the hotel. Tip: When parking in the deck, the restaurant only validates for 2 hours.

Taqueria del Sol, 1200 Howell Mill Rd. Northwest, Atlanta, GA 30318; (404) 352-5811; www.taqueriadelsol.com; Mexican; $. Nominated for a James Beard award in the Outstanding Restaurateur category, Taqueria del Sol keeps the crowds coming back for tasty and cheap food. What's really great about the restaurant is that they are able to mix in authentic Mexican flavors into their food but still have wide appeal. In addition, since the items are a la carte, prices are kept extremely low. Don't be deterred by the long lines that form outside the restaurant. The line moves quickly as food is delivered to parties in a short amount of time. It's a house rule not to grab a table until your food is ready; however, this is rarely problematic as most eat quickly and leave, turning tables over in a hurry. Start with the amazing cheese dip and shrimp-and-corn chowder. Order the fish or fried chicken tacos with lime-jalapeño mayonnaise. Pork tacos with barbecue sauce and coleslaw are highly addictive, too. Margaritas are excellent and prepared with the perfect mix of tequila and sweet stuff, so don't miss out on trying one. This is a perfect place for a small group of 4 to 6 people to grab a quick meal. Tip: If you are on your own, avoid the line altogether and sit at the bar.

Top FLR, 674 Myrtle St. Northeast, Atlanta, GA 30308; (404) 685-3110; www.topflr.com; American; $$. With an outstanding and inventive drink menu and a hipster vibe, many liken Atlanta's Top FLR to the intimate and unique restaurants in New York City. Tucked away on a side street in Midtown, it could easily be missed unless you are looking for it, but it's absolutely worth seeking out this unique part-bar, part-restaurant establishment. Stepping inside, don't be put off by the somewhat basic-looking surroundings. The cocktail menu has classics like a gimlet, old-fashioned, French 75, and Pimm's Cup, but why not try one of the rotating concoctions such as the Strange Horse or Rhubarbella, which are all expertly crafted. The food will impress here, too. Start your meal with the tuna tartare on Sardinian flatbread: The fresh avocado and arugula was a winning flavor combination. For entrees order the duck pizza or the hanger steak. Be careful to read the menu, as many dishes don't come with sides, and they must be ordered separately. The mac 'n' cheese is scrumptious with a mix of Gouda, panko crust, and slight spice; it the perfect companion to the hanger steak. The restaurant is a perfect date spot or for a small gathering; it becomes dimly lit and highly romantic after dark. Tip: It serves late into the evening.

West Egg Cafe, 1100 Howell Mill Rd. Northwest, Atlanta, GA 30318; (404) 872-3973; www.westeggcafe.com; Breakfast/Brunch/ Lunch; $. West Egg is known for phenomenal cupcakes, and most visitors can't resist picking up at least one on their way out. With flavors like red velvet, and hummingbird, they deliver a lot of flavor in a small portion. While the menu has many breakfast and brunch favorites, there is a decidedly Southern slant to their options. Items like butter bean hummus, collard greens, and fried green tomatoes are prominent on the menu. West Egg Cafe is open for breakfast, lunch, and dinner; however, dinner has a somewhat limited menu. Good to note that they do serve breakfast all day long. Lunch favorites include the Redneck Reuben, which is turkey soaked in sweet tea, coleslaw is substituted for sauerkraut, and it's topped off with Coca-Cola barbecue sauce. Brunch favorites include the short rib hash and the *huevos tejanos* (scrambled eggs with jalapeño, chipotle salsa, and sour cream). They offer free Wi-Fi, and many patrons are regulars who live and work in the area. Tip: On Wednesday, you can get a double burger and your choice of a beer or a milk shake for only $10. Plenty of free parking is available in the deck behind the restaurant.

Landmarks

Antico Pizza, 1093 Hemphill Ave., Atlanta, GA 30318; (404) 873-1272; http://anticopizza.it; Pizza; $$. Antico sits in a small, nondescript building on the outskirts of Midtown. Touted as one of the best pizzas in the city, the Neopolitan pizza uses very fresh ingredients; in fact, many are imported directly from Italy. The ovens are even from Italy. Antico was brought to fame by a couple bloggers who extolled its exquisite pizza. In the blink of an eye, it was an overnight sensation, and they continue to satisfy pizza enthusiasts. They are so popular that they now continue to make pizza each day until they run out of dough. A unique feature of the "restaurant" is that there isn't a dining room per se. There are long wooden picnic tables that were brought into the kitchen for diners to eat at, because it was never really intended to be a restaurant. But diners now can sit at these communal tables and watch as their pizzas are made before their eyes, served up piping hot after coming out of the 1,000-degree oven. While the Margherita pizza

ATLANTA'S SECRET SUPPERS

Secret suppers are one of the trendiest things going on in Atlanta besides the food truck movement. There are several secret suppers and underground foodie events that go on throughout the city. Like **Black Tie Barbecue** (below), the locations remain secret until the day before the event. With some diligent research you can easily find out about these secret events and be added to their e-mail list, but in order to keep the magic and mystery about them, we won't disclose that information in this book. But they are well worth seeking out. **Black Tie Barbecue** (http://black-tie-barbecue.com) was started by two couples. The husbands—laid-off management consultants—took their love of cooking and started a catering company that has become wildly successful. With an operation in the downtown area they offer lunch service (pickup only) on Friday. The name Black Tie was carefully chosen to take something they both love and elevate it to a higher standard. Besides offering takeaway lunch options, they started the Secret Suppers as a way to spread the word about their catering business. They are at unique locations only disclosed the day before the event. All food is served family-style, which facilitates getting to know your neighbors. These secret suppers take place 5 to 6 times per year and sell out quickly. Get on their mailing list to be notified when tickets go on sale.

is a customer favorite, don't miss out on the diavola (spicy peppers and sopressata) and the San Gennaro (sausage with sweet peppers).

Bacchanalia, 1198 Howell Mill Rd., Ste. 100, Atlanta, GA 30318; (404) 365-0410; www.starprovisions.com; Contemporary American; $$$$. Bacchanalia is about an experience, not just food or service (both of which are exceptional). The crowd tends to be upwards of 40, mainly due to the hefty price tag that comes with dining here. Chef-Owners Anne Quatrano and Clifford Harrison's culinary philosophy is to create light dishes built on strong flavors. The menu is seasonal, using organic and locally sourced items. By local, we mean sourced from Anne and Clifford's farm. For starters, get the crab fritter if it is available, as it is nearly all lump crab. Menu items may include the charcuterie plate consisting of 6 items: pork rillette, duck, ham with onion relish, Ungherese (a type of salami), house-cured *lonzino* (a cured pork loin) with *chicharrones* (pork rinds, or fried pork skins), and summer sausage or Moulard duck, served over glazed parsnips with a duck liver crostini. It is always rated one of Atlanta's top restaurants and has been the number one restaurant in the Zagat guide since 1996. The restaurant offers a 4-course prix-fixe menu composed of appetizer, entree, cheese, and dessert. Closed Sunday.

JCT Kitchen, 1198 Howell Mill Rd., Ste. 18, Atlanta, GA 30318; (404) 355-2252; www.jctkitchen.com; Southern; $$$$. There is a complex in the West Midtown area that is a little off the beaten path but houses some of the most-talked-about restaurants in the city. One of the restaurants that makes its home here is JCT Kitchen. Under the direction of Ford Fry, JCT Kitchen turns out some incredibly tasty dishes with a slightly Southern spin. The Angry Mussels, cooked up with bacon, were once featured on the Food Network, so it remains a must-try for many who visit the restaurant. One of the most popular dishes on the menu is fried chicken. Although a simple dish, it keeps folks coming back over and over again. However, one of the best dishes on the menu is the rabbit; cooked to perfection, it is moist and tender. Trout is another standout dish. The restaurant also has a line of "haute" dogs that are available each day, and on Wednesday (dubbed Wiener Wednesday) they are available for only $2. There's also a lovely rooftop patio that is fun for socializing and even has live music on certain nights. (Tip: Since the parking lot serves many other restaurants, it gets full fast. However, there is ample free parking to be found in the parking deck located across the bridge from the restaurant, and it is a short and pleasant walk.)

Mary Mac's Tea Room, 224 Ponce de Leon Ave., Atlanta, GA 30308; (404) 876-1800; www.marymacs.com; Southern; $$. Mary Mac's is one of the truly iconic restaurants that have graced Atlanta for many years. Back in the 1940s, there were 16 tearooms in Atlanta. Although not a place that served tea, these were a fancied-up versions of a meat and three. They were centers for neighborhoods where families could go and enjoy good food in the company of friends. Today Mary Mac's is the only tearoom that remains in Atlanta. Mary Mac's has had its doors open for 65 years, serving up classic Southern food to famous celebrities like Richard Gere, Beyoncé, and Paula Deen. Even some of the servers have been there for decades. It is an early crowd at Mary Mac's, with customers starting to enter at 4 p.m. Although a signature drink is the peach martini, don't visit without sampling their sweet tea, which was featured in *Travel + Leisure* magazine. Everything on the menu is quite tasty, like fried okra, salmon cakes, fried green tomatoes, fried chicken tenders, fried crawfish, and ribs. Tip: All first-time guests are treated to a sample Pot Likker—go and find out what it is!

Nan Thai Fine Dining, 1350 Spring St., Atlanta, GA 30309; (404) 870-9933; www.nanfinedining.com; Thai; $$$$. The ambience of Nan is utterly unforgettable. From the giant golden tamarind outside to the rattan-style furniture inside and the servers wearing traditional attire, attention to detail is evident. Everything relating to design and aesthetics is well-planned and is very eye-catching. The interior also features an open kitchen displaying herbs and spices. It is truly beautiful inside this Atlanta favorite. Nan is the sister restaurant to longtime Thai favorite **Tamarind Seed** (p. 97), also located in Midtown. Two of the best menu items are the steamed sea bass and lamb. The fish on a bed of bok choy is perfectly complemented by the use of ginger. The New Zealand lamb chops are flawlessly cooked, and the subtle seasoning lets most of the lamb flavor come through. If you really want to splurge, go for the Chef's Table: $115 per person inclusive of wine pairings. It includes 8 courses (3 apps, 1 salad, 1 soup, 2 entrees, and 1 dessert). Service is definitely top-notch, and the presentation is beautiful. Tip: Take a peek inside the restroom; it is truly beautiful with the natural stone waterfall sink.

ONE. Midtown Kitchen, 559 Dutch Valley Rd. Northeast, Atlanta, GA 30324; (404) 892-4111; www.onemidtownkitchen.com American; $$$. Part of the Concentrics Restaurant Empire, ONE. Midtown Kitchen opened back in 2002 and was an immediate success. Nearly a decade later, the allure of the neon sign, its swanky bar scene, and modern look still make ONE. Midtown Kitchen a pretty hot Atlanta destination. The bar scene is a destination all by itself; with its wall of wines and specialty cocktails, it can make for a fun couple's evening or girls' night out. Every wine is available by the half glass, glass, bottle, and bottomless (call a cab!). Wines are categorized into 4 price tiers. These options allow guests to sample different wines throughout their meal—all for one price. Start your meal off with their calamari. It may sound trite, but theirs is truly unique. Instead of the thin rounds you'll get everywhere else, these are thick tubes of calamari. Pastas are house-made and can be ordered in half or full portions. Meats and vegetables used in pasta dishes change regularly to keep dishes interesting. Pork entrees are all highlights. Desserts are small but decadent, so don't overlook them!

Park 75, 75 14th St., Atlanta, GA 30309; (404) 253-3840; www
.fourseasons.com/atlanta/dining/park_75; American; $$$$. Park 75
is located in the Four Seasons Hotel, and this restaurant is top-
notch. Stepping inside, one immediately gets a feeling of regality;
however, it isn't stuffy. Service is pleasant and attentive. The
kitchen can address special dietary needs such as gluten intolerance
very easily. There's a nod to Southern cuisine with starters like pork
belly and mains of shrimp and grits. Brunch selections are amazing.
The seafood selections at brunch—tuna tartare, oysters, crabs, and
more—are extremely fresh. A unique brunch feature is
their mini potpies with choice of lamb, beef, chicken,
or lobster. The coffee is brewed just right. However,
make sure to start brunch off with a Bloody Mary;
Park 75 serves up their rather large one in a mason
jar, another nod to the South.

Quinones at Bacchanalia, 1198 Howell Mill Rd., Atlanta, GA
30318; (404) 365-0410; www.starprovisions.com; American; $$$$.
Bacchanalia (p. 102) is consistently rated one of the top restaurants in Atlanta. Well, Quinones is even more upscale. Think nicer
linens and decor. You'll find mostly couples celebrating a special
occasion like an anniversary or birthday. There are numerous dinner
courses, so plan to spend 3 or more hours. While the cuisine isn't
the most innovative or creative, it is flawlessly prepared and perfectly executed. The waitstaff is among the most professional in
Atlanta. They cater to your every need, making this not just a meal,
but an experience. Having said that, be ready to pay for it.

Silver Skillet, 200 14th St. Northwest, Atlanta, GA 30318; (404) 874-1388; www.thesilverskillet.com; Diner; $. This Atlanta institution, in business for over 55 years, was featured on Food Network's *Diners, Drive-Ins and Dives*. To experience a Southern breakfast in an Atlanta landmark, look no further. The biscuits and grits (staples in any good Southern breakfast) and pork chop breakfast are spectacular. Servers are friendly, and the place has a cozy, nostalgic feel. (Note: Silver Skillet closes around 2 p.m.)

Sublime Doughnuts, 535 10th St. Northwest, Atlanta, GA 30318; (404) 897-1801; www.sublimedoughnuts.com; Bakery; $. Here, some would argue, are some of the best doughnuts in Atlanta. Sublime Doughnuts was started by Atlanta resident Kamal Grant. After studying at the Culinary Institute of America in New York, Grant soon found his calling to be making pastries.

In fact, the Sublime Doughnuts are so delicious and complex in flavor, they are more like pastries. Try the strawberries-and-cream, made with real strawberries, or the Orange Dream Star, with its sweet but light orange glaze. The Reese's Peanut Butter Cup and dulce de leche are also customer favorites.

Veni Vidi Vici, 41 14th St., Atlanta, GA 30309; (404) 875-8424; www.buckheadliferestaurants.com; Italian; $$$$. The literal translation is "I came, I saw, I conquered." It is beautiful inside, and the high ceilings and light-colored decor make the place appear even bigger than it is. It is perfect for a couple's night on the town, for a business dinner, or even for a family celebrating a special occasion. Starters that should not be missed are the calamari and the octopus. The calamari is a rather large portion, and one order will be plenty for a table of four. Suckling pig and veal chop entrees are menu highlights. Seafood lovers will enjoy the risotto frutti di mare: fresh shrimp, mussels, clams, and calamari served up in a creamy risotto mixture. Vegetarians won't miss out with the gnocchi di patate—potato gnocchi with Parmesan cream. Soft and creamy, it can be enjoyed by meat eaters as well. The portions are rather large, and pastas are available in the half size. Although the restaurant can be pricey, they often offer a prix-fixe menu under $30.

Woody's Cheesesteaks, 981 Monroe Dr. Northeast, Atlanta, GA 30308; (404) 876-1939; Sandwiches; $. The tiny operation cranks out some of the tastiest cheesesteaks on this side of the Mason-Dixon Line. True Philadelphians might say they are not completely authentic, but this rather tiny hut has quite a following, so be prepared to wait a while for your sandwich. Everything is cooked to order. Of course they offer other sandwiches and hot dogs, but the star of the show here is the cheesesteak. Get the All the Way with onions and ketchup, or load it up with mushrooms and banana peppers. Either way, you won't regret it. The parking lot is small, but when available, there's a quaint little outdoor eating area. They've recently begun to accept credit cards and now are open into the wee hours of the mornings on the weekends (until 4 a.m. Fri and Sat).

Bakeshop, 903 Peachtree St., Ste. C, Atlanta, GA 30309; (404) 892-9322; www.bakeshopatl.com; Bakery; $. Bakeshop has all the qualities of a neighborhood bakery and a great atmosphere that encourages lounging—Wi-Fi, complimentary newspapers, and communal tables that encourage conversing with others. The small bakery is self-serve. Grab the pastry or item you'd like, then order coffee at the register. Breakfast outshines lunch, although sandwiches are fresh. Tables have Nutella available to tempt guests. Do not visit without sampling the chocolate-almond croissant. (Tip: They feature monthly BYO Bakeshop Dinners where you bring your own alcohol. The dinners are 3 courses for $40, which includes tax, gratuity, and the corkage fee. Entrees include short ribs, skirt steak, and fried chicken.)

Star Provisions, 1198 Howell Mill Rd., Atlanta, GA 30318; (404) 365-0410; www.starprovisions.com; Specialty market; $$. This market features cheeses, wines, beer, meats, seafood, and many other gourmet food items. Stop here to buy fresh cuts of meat or get that obscure cheese (they have over 200 varieties). Staff is very knowledgeable and can help you choose based on taste preferences. Tim, the resident cheesemonger, is quite capable and helpful when it comes to recommendations, so don't miss talking to him. They also have cookware and gadgets that make it a foodie's paradise. Star Provisions also serves up some tasty sandwiches, albeit a bit pricey but very high on quality. They boast one of the best shrimp po'boys, and their Reuben is also a menu highlight.

Toscano and Sons, 1000 Marietta St., Ste. 105, Atlanta, GA 30318; (404) 815-8383; www.toscanoandsons.com; Italian; $. This specialty Italian market serves up some very tasty sandwiches as well as hard to find, fresh Italian goods. The sandwiches, or paninis, are made fresh while you wait, and are quite filling and under $5. The Italian meats and cheeses are stuffed inside the crusty ciabatta bread, pressed, and served warm. Try the namesake Toscano made with sopressata, fontina cheese, and arugula, or the Viola with mortadella, speck salami, provolone, and tapenade. Stock up on Italian goods like pastas, olive oils, wines, deli meats, and more. It is a favorite of nearby office workers and has few tables, so many take their sandwiches to go. Plenty of parking in the parking deck attached.

Gwinnett/Decatur

Gwinnett County is a suburb of the metro area. Much like Cobb County, it is part of the urban sprawl that occurred in Atlanta over the last 15 years. During one point in that time frame, Gwinnett was one of the fastest growing counties in the nation. One difference between Cobb and Gwinnett is the large ethnic communities that are prevalent in the latter. There are lots of Korean and other Asian nationalities represented, as well as a large Hispanic population.

Although the two towns are in fairly close proximity, Decatur is quite different from Gwinnett. Decatur is located inside the perimeter, or what Atlantans refer to as ITP, versus Gwinnett being OTP. What Decatur residents love about their city is that it has the small town feel, but it is extremely close to all the amenities the city has to offer. Many fine dining and unique establishments have located in Decatur. Even those who aren't residents make the drive to experience this friendly, easygoing yet hip city.

Armando's Caribe, 3170 Peachtree Industrial Blvd., Ste. 195, Duluth, GA 30097; (770) 232-9848; http://armandoscaribe.com; Latin; $$. House specials are *paella de mariscos,* or shrimp paella, which also comes with calamari, salmon, scallops, and mussels as well. Even though the tendency would be to gravitate toward the more traditional seafood paella, don't overlook the *paella valenciana,* with pork strips marinated in a mango vinaigrette, which is an unusual take on paella. Regulars also rave about the lobster tacos. Potato-crusted calamari frito is a good start to the meal, as is the yuca frita. At lunch a traditional Cuban sandwich is tasty, but the Ruben Cubano, chicken marinated in *mojo criollo* sauce, is better. Don't forget to save room for the delicious house-made flan. Daily specials under $10.

Bhojanic, 1363 Clairmont Rd., Decatur, GA 30033; (404) 633-9233; www.bhojanic.com; Indian; $$. Although the decor is somewhat minimalist at Bhojanic, it works well for the space. This Indian restaurant has the decor of a slick and trendy place that you may find in Midtown, but that doesn't affect the quality or the authenticity of the food. Portions are pretty large, especially for the *thali,* which is large enough for two meals. Don't miss out their mango lassi, vegetable samosa, or chicken tikka masala. The paneer tikka, which is basically a type of Indian cheese served up with a mint chutney, is extremely tasty. You'll want to place several orders for the garlic naan, as it comes hot and fresh and disappears rather quickly. For those who enjoy hot and spicy, order the chicken 65. Bhojanic is also family friendly. Closed Sunday.

Bukharaa Indian, 3651-F Peachtree Pkwy., Suwanee, GA 30097; (770) 817-1371; www.bukharaa.com; Indian; $$. The best way to experience this North Indian restaurant, located up in Suwanee, is to give the buffet a try. Whether ordering from the menu or buffet make sure to try the paneer tikka masala; the texture is pleasing as is the creamy taste. Staff is friendly and helpful and, during the lunch buffet, is sure to come by with fresh, hot naan to complement the various lunch offerings. Lamb lovers will especially be pleased with the lamb *rogan josh*. On the other hand, those who want hot and spicy, rest assured their vindaloo is tasty yet sweat-inducing. Other favorites are the butter chicken (wonderfully creamy) and chicken 65. Entrees are cooked to order and can take longer than in most restaurants, but they are worth the wait. So it is recommended to order some appetizers while waiting for mains to be served.

Burnt Fork BBQ, 614 Church St., Decatur, GA 30030; (404) 373-7155; www.burntforkbbq.com; Barbecue; $$. This barbecue joint had to be very confident to open up within several miles of three or four of the top barbecue restaurants in the city. Given that, it certainly holds its own. One of the reasons it is favored is the variety of barbecue regions covered by the sauces offered: There's Memphis (sweet), Kansas City (smoky), North Carolina (vinegar based), and South Carolina (mustard based). The pulled pork with its slight smokiness is tasty, as is the brisket. The restaurant bakes its own bread for sandwiches, so it is worth ordering a sandwich to enjoy the fresh bread that goes with it. Mac 'n' cheese and the coleslaw are probably the best sides. The knives, forks, and take-out boxes are all green-friendly. Closed Sunday.

Cafe Todahmgol, 2442 Pleasant Hill Rd., #3B, Duluth, GA 30096; (770) 813-8202; Korean; $$. This restaurant serves Korean food and is patronized by many Koreans, but few Americans. Menus are not in English and servers speak very little, if any, English, though they try to be as helpful as possible. Adventurous eaters must make do by pointing at pictures on the menu. Order the *galbi* (short ribs) and the *gyeop sal* (pork belly). It is a good idea to go with a group, as you'll get to sample a good selection of different meats. The *banchan,* or sides, that accompany dinner are plentiful as well and include rice, tofu soup, peppers, kimchee, pickled radish, and carrots on ice. Note: They allow indoor smoking, so those who are sensitive to cigarettes may want to avoid this place.

Cakes & Ale, 254 W. Ponce de Leon Ave., Decatur, GA 30030; (770) 377-7994; http://cakesandalerestaurant.com; American; $$$. Don't let the name fool you: they are not big on cakes or ale.

Instead the restaurant gets its name from a famous term coined by Shakespeare that means "all good things in life." This small restaurant tucked into a corner of some busy streets in Decatur does quite the business, even more since it was written up on Eater.com as one of the hottest spots to visit in Atlanta. The restaurant is big on using locally sourced items, and as such the menu changes frequently. Start your meal off with the flavorful and savory *arancini*. The focus tends to be on using the finest local ingredients to make superb dishes. Think potato gnocchi with cauliflower and pumpkin-seed pesto. For dessert, don't miss out on the Phatty Cakes. They also make creative cocktails like the habañero gimlet. The space is small, and reservations are recommended for any night of the week.

Chicken and Beer (BBQ Chicken), 3473 Old Norcross Rd., Duluth, GA 30096; (678) 417-6464; www.bbqchickenatl.com; Korean Chicken; $. Seeing this restaurant's name, some would come to the obvious conclusion that this is an establishment that serves barbecue chicken; they would be wrong. In this case, "BBQ" stands for "best of the best quality." This is a Korean fried chicken restaurant. Start your meal with the crispy fried green beans; the batter is so light, it is like a tempura batter. Their signature dish is the chicken deep-fried in olive oil. It is coated in a blend of 30 spices for a unique flavor. Order that with a side of their delicious waffle fries. The menu also includes wings, grilled chicken, and sandwiches.

Community Q, 1361 Clairmont Rd., North Decatur, GA 30033; (404) 633-2080; www.communityqbbq.com; Barbecue; $$. This is easily one of the most popular barbecue restaurants in the city. Fans rave about the pulled pork with its smoky flavor and the tasty brisket. Ribs are juicy and full of meat, and almost don't need either of the two sauces that are found on the tables: sweet and vinegar based. The mac 'n' cheese side gets high marks, too. While the wait may not be super long, do expect a 15- to 20-minute wait on weekends. Note that there isn't table service here. Diners place and pay for orders at the counter; food is brought to their table shortly. Note that the restaurant closes quite early—8:30 p.m. on weekdays and 9:30 p.m. on weekends.

East Pearl Seafood, 1810 Liddell Ln., Duluth, GA 30098; (678) 380-0899; Dim Sum; $$. For a consistent quality dim sum, East Pearl is the spot to visit. The only caveat is that they do get quite busy and go through their dim sum quite fast on weekends, so it is best to come before noon. Otherwise, you might be eating dim sum that isn't the freshest. When you do have the fresh dim sum, it is worth it, especially the shrimp and pork. It is set up with large tables so it's great for groups. Tip: If you have a favorite type of tea, bring some, and they will brew a pot for you. No "baggage" fees.

Farmburger, 410B W. Ponce de Leon, Decatur, GA 30030; (404) 378-5077; www.farmburger.net; Burgers; $$. Newly opened,

Farmburger was an instant success from the time the doors opened. This burger spot in the Decatur neighborhood is different because the ingredients are organic and locally sourced. Fans are more than happy to pay a few extra dollars to help support local economies. The decor is simple, not chic or trendy like some of the newer burger joints tend to be. While it offers up mostly indoor seating, there are a few tables outside. Burgers are grass fed, and the taste comes through and is in no way dwarfed by any of the toppings. Customers can build their own burger or order one of the specialty burgers. Unique toppings include oxtail marmalade and roasted bone marrow. Do try the house-made pickles. For sides, choose onion rings over the fries. Lines can be extremely long. Visit during off-peak times for quicker service.

Grace 17.20, 5155 Peachtree Pkwy., Norcross, GA 30092; (678) 421-1720; www.grace1720.com; American; $$$$. The name Grace 17.20 comes from the Bible verse Matthew 17:20, but the religious overtones end there. The interior is beautifully appointed with white tablecloths and a light and bright color on the walls. The large windows add the bright and cheery ambience. Once seated inside you forget you are in a strip mall shopping center. When weather allows, patrons like to dine alfresco, as the patio has a certain Tuscan charm about it, especially during a lazy Sunday afternoon. Wine and drinks are very tasty, but can be on the pricey side. The complimentary pumpkin bread that is served with meals is a favorite of many. Start with the spicy chicken spring rolls. Soups like chilled pea and tomato chipotle are always popular. Among main courses, the marbled pork chop with collards and grits has long been one of the most-ordered entrees.

Haru Ichiban, 3646 Satellite Blvd., Duluth, GA 30096; (770) 622-4060; www.haruichibanjapaneserestaurant.com; Japanese/Sushi; $$. Patrons drive very far out of their way to eat at this sushi restaurant. It is a favorite of Japanese, who make up about three-quarters of the clientele. There are lunch specials each day, and the sashimi offers some high-quality ingredients. Ramen here is quite exceptional, too. Try the *chasu* or the *tonkatsu* ramen. The extensive menu also includes cold noodles, tempura, and rice dishes, so there's certainly something to suit all kinds of palates.

Iberian Pig, 121 Sycamore St., Decatur, GA 30030; (404) 371-8800; www.theiberianpigatl.com; Spanish/Mediterranean; $$$. As the name suggests, this is a Spanish/Mediterranean restaurant. Located in close proximity to Decatur Square, it is a favorite of many who live in the neighborhood. The restaurant gets its name from the black-footed Iberian pigs from which the restaurant's signature item, *jamón ibérico,* a cured meat, originate. There's a good selection of meats and cheeses, but the appetizers offer much more in the way of flavor. In fact, many groups treat these as tapas, not ordering any main courses. Bacon-wrapped dates and pork cheek tacos are popular starters. For a more complex appetizer, order the *albóndigas*—wild boar meatballs stuffed with piquillo peppers, dates, and tomatoes. Skip seafood dishes in favor of meat entrees.

Highlights are the Moscatel filet, beef tenderloin topped with manchego cheese, dates, walnuts, even bacon. Another menu highlight is the cabrito carbonara—slow-roasted goat topped with pasta tossed in a carbonara sauce and a poached egg.

Las Brasas, 310 E. Howard Ave., Decatur, GA 30030; (404) 377-9121; www.lasbrasasdecatur.com; Latin; $. Forget those grocery store rotisserie chickens and head over to this popular Decatur spot to pick up some Peruvian-spiced rotisserie chicken. The spot is tiny and takeout only. The restaurant can hold about 5 people, and there are only a couple parking spots available. However, that doesn't stop its loyal customers from lining up for this uniquely addictive chicken. The skin is crispy, and the meat remains juicy. Order chicken by the quarter, half, and full size. The combo meals come with your choice of side: corn on the cob, fried tortilla chips and avocado dip, pinto beans and rice, french fries, or sweet potato fries. Round out your meal with an Inca Kola, a Peruvian soft drink. Closed Sunday.

Leon's Full Service, 131 E. Ponce de Leon Ave., Decatur, GA 30030; (404) 687-0500 http://leonsfullservice.com; Gastropub; $$$. This Decatur neighborhood pub has gained much acclaim in several years since it has been open. There's a unique offering of microbrews on draft, which change out regularly. The cocktail list is also inventive and changes seasonally. Expect cocktails like the pisco sling, which is made with house Falernum liqueur and green Chartreuse. Start a meal with their famous pub frites; these tasty fries are paired with your sauce of choice (14 to choose from). With flavors like goat cheese fondue, madras curry ketchup, or bacon and tarragon mayonnaise, they are delightful. Don't miss the house-made sausages and charcuterie plate. A side of brussels sprout hash with bacon, onion, and apple is tasty and creative. Skip expensive entrees and opt for sandwiches, which are every bit as tasty. Try the brisket or burger. Snag patio seating when the weather allows. Note: Large tables are hard to come by, so this is better for small groups or couples. Reservations not accepted.

Maddy's, 1479 Scott Blvd., Decatur, GA 30030; (404) 377-0401; www.maddysribs.com; Barbecue; $$. Maddy's has been in the Atlanta area for quite some time now, before barbecue became trendy. There is live blues music scheduled each night, so blues and barbecue fans should most definitely put this on their itinerary. The menu is rather small, but what they do churn out is quite good. The top items are the pulled pork sandwich and the barbecue ribs. For sides skip the bland mac 'n' cheese in favor of the Brunswick stew or rum baked beans, both extraordinary. Tip: They allow patrons to BYOB.

Naan N Curry, 3083 Breckinridge Blvd.; (770) 912-9924; Indian; $. Located in the Gwinnett Place area, this no-frills restaurant is a perfect place to stop in for a quick meal while running errands in the area. Lunch is buffet only. Order off the menu for dinner options. Two of the menu highlights are the chicken tikka masala and the chicken biryani. Vegetarians will enjoy the chana masala. They even serve a couple ground beef entrees: *nehari* and *haleem*. Naan is served light, hot, and fluffy. Note that this establishment serves food with lots of spice. So those who enjoy milder foods may not be able to stand the heat of these entrees. For the price, it is one of the best values to be had in the area.

Pastas and Tapas, 9700 Medlock Bridge Rd., Ste. 186, Duluth, GA 30097; (770) 497-0083; www.pastasandtapas.com; Italian/Spanish; $$. A rare combination of Italian and Spanish foods, Pastas and Tapas has carved out its own niche in the metro Atlanta area. A combination of house-made pastas complemented by unique sauces is matched with authentic Spanish tapas. Owner Tony Vitulli is there most of the time, greeting customers, and the entire staff makes you feel like family. Pricing and portions are small enough, so try many dishes. Start with one of the salads: *Spinaci* with strawberries, spinach, and feta is a hit, as is the *jamón serrano* with ham and arugula in orange vinaigrette. For pastas try the lasagna or the gnocchi with a simple pomodoro sauce. Also, the paella marinara is one of the most popular dishes, but allow 30 minutes for preparation. For tapas try the garlic shrimp and calamari. Don't miss out on the tiramisu for dessert.

Pearl Lian Oriental Bistro and Bakery, 11600 Medlock Bridge Rd., Duluth, GA 30097; (678) 205-1326; www.pearl-lian.com; Asian; $$. This well-appointed restaurant is somewhat of a hodgepodge of Asian foods. There's Japanese, Chinese, and Thai all to be found on the menu. The decor is a little more high-end than what would be expected from most Chinese restaurants, with its tall ceilings, stone bar, and upscale atmosphere, and the food is consistently on point. Start with an order of basil rolls, prepared excellently. The tangerine beef has been one of the most popular items for years, but the sesame seed–crusted tuna is quite popular as well. There's a pretty extensive lunch menu for the express lunch, served weekdays, with the sweet lime curry being one of the standouts. During the evening, sit at the bar before dinner and give the Asian pear martini a try.

Raging Burrito, 141 Sycamore St., Decatur, GA 30030; (404) 377-3311; www.ragingburrito.com; Mexican; $. Patrons don't just flock to Raging Burrito for the delicious Tex-Mex food, but also for their terrific beer selection (16 on draft), outstanding margaritas, and the lovely patio that is in high demand during optimal weather. This spot consistently has some of the best fish tacos in the city. To get a sampling of different meats, tacos are the best bet. In addition to fish, try the brisket and chipotle. Burritos can be customized with choice of meat, vegetables, and fillers. They do offer unique choices like the pineapple jerk, Bangkok, or Tokyo Teriyaki burrito. Tip: Although the restaurant offers validated parking in the adjacent lot, it is often full at peak hours, but other parking can be found on nearby side streets.

Saba, 350 Meade Rd., Decatur, GA 30030; (404) 377-9266; www .saba-restaurant.com; Italian; $$. Made up of pastas and sandwiches, Saba's primarily Italian menu has some unique offerings like Thai ravioli with peanut and cilantro sauce, as well as vindaloo tofu spaghetti. Saba is a great restaurant for vegetarians, as there are lots of vegetarian options on their menu. The pumpkin ravioli makes a good vegetarian entree but could easily double as a good appetizer for 2 or 3 to share. It is a good choice, with its slightly sweet brown-butter glaze. Another standout entree is the huge and hearty sausage sandwich—ground sausage with onions and red peppers served on 2 fresh ciabatta buns. (Tip: The restaurant is kid-friendly in the early evening hours. Later on it becomes more like a bar with live music on weekends.)

Sun in My Belly, 2161 College Ave., Atlanta, GA 30317; (404) 370-1088; www.suninmybelly.com; Breakfast/Lunch; $$. This kitschy restaurant, located in a primarily residential part of town, used to be a hardware store. In fact, they left the old signage up at the restaurant entrance. So, keep your eyes peeled for the sign that says HARDWARE STORE if you are visiting for the first time and relying on your GPS. The decor is very basic and sparse: there's butcher paper on the tables and drinks are served out of mason jars. There are a couple of couches for lounging. Coffees are served in large

mugs and are so tasty that they make guests want
to surf their laptops while sipping. Breakfast,
brunch, and lunch are served. The cumin-spiked
hummus is not to be missed. This smoky hummus
with pita points is tasty and perfect for sharing. The
Kirkwood breakfast of scrambled eggs with Boursin
cheese is another hit, served with bacon and a good-as-Grandma-
used-to-make biscuit. Sweets lovers should get the challah french
toast. With its honeyed ricotta and berries, it is quite indulgent.
During lunch, the fried green tomato sandwich with bacon and
pimiento cheese is a hearty and yummy treat, as is the Napoleon
Complex with brie, prosciutto, and fig jam. Note: They also have
a satellite location in the Atlanta Botanical Gardens. Tip: Bring
your own bubbly and make your own mimosas at lunch (no corkage
fees).

Trattoria one 41, 9810 Medlock Bridge Rd., Ste. A, Johns Creek,
GA 30097; (770) 497-0021; www.trattoria141.com; Italian; $$.
Upon being seated, servers bring patrons bread to start with a mari-
nara sauce with bits of goat cheese in it that is divine. But don't
fill up on that, as appetizers and entrees are decent-size portions,
and you'll want to save room. Start with the mussels or artichoke
appetizer. Notable entrees are the veal chop, a huge portion that
is perfectly cooked, as well as the *vongole,* which is a clam pasta
dish. Neither will disappoint. Gnocchi is quite solid as well. Service
is friendly and professional. Open for dinner daily. It gets busy on
weekends. Reservations recommended. Note: Most patrons dress

up for dinner here, so you may want to leave the jeans and tennis shoes at home.

Zapata, 15 Jones St., Norcross, GA 30071; (770)248-0052; www .zapata-atl.com; Mexican; $$. Named after Emiliano Zapata, the most legendary leader of the Mexican Revolution, Zapata strives to be one of the most authentic restaurants in the area. Their signature dish is *molcajetes,* which is a meal cooked in a volcanic stone pot. It comes with fresh tomatillo sauce, and nopal, a Mexican flat cactus. Other standout dishes are the enchiladas or chicken breast topped with mole sauce. This is a sauce made with chocolate, nuts, and a myriad of other spices. At lunch, order the authentic *chilaquiles,* a traditional meal of tortilla strips cooked with shredded chicken and topped with cheese and sour cream.

Landmarks

Athens Pizza, 1341 Clairmont Rd., Ste. A, Decatur, GA 30033; (404) 636-1100 www.athenspizzaatlanta.com; Pizza; $$.. Calling this establishment a pizza joint is a bit of a misnomer. This is a full-on restaurant with appetizers, salads, wraps, subs, and Italian and Greek entrees. So while they are quite famous for their pizza, it is important not to overlook the fact that a group could dine here and each individual could have something different. The pizza is unique in that there is definitely a Greek slant to it. Try the Athens special with feta cheese, meats, mushrooms, onions, and peppers. Or try the Santorini special, a vegetarian pizza with feta, sun-dried tomatoes, spinach, garlic, artichoke hearts, and olives. There are specials each night of the week except Saturday. These include moussaka or lamb shank with orzo pasta. Tip: Lunch specials are a great deal at under $10. Try the gyro wrap, eggplant parmigiana, or personal pizza with one topping.

Brick Store Pub, 125 E. Court Sq., Decatur, GA 30030; (404) 687-0990; www.brickstorepub.com; Pub; $. Located in the heart of Decatur, it is hard to miss the Brick Store Pub. The decor is brick walls and a wood bar, tables, and stools. Of the two levels of the pub, the bottom tends to be much more open and less crowded, while the top is where most like to congregate. It's extremely popular with Decatur residents and those living even further away, so expect a full house no matter what night of the week it is. As one can imagine the beer list is extensive, and Belgian-beer lovers will be glad to know that these brews are a specialty here. While, it is a pub first, the food is nothing to sneeze at. The menu isn't large but what they make, they make quite well. Start with hummus or pierogies. Skip burgers in favor of sandwiches, especially the chicken salad melt, made with dates, pine nuts, and cream cheese, and served on wheat-berry bread. For entrees the house special fish-and-chips is served hot and crispy and lives up to its reputation, and the classic shepherd's pie is given a twist with a mixture of lamb, beef, and pork, mixed with gruyère sauce and mesclun greens.

Cafe Alsace, 121 E. Ponce de Leon Ave., Decatur, GA 30030; (404) 373-5622; www.cafealsace.net; French; $$. This tiny French restaurant located near Decatur Square is easy to miss, so be on the lookout. The quaint and cozy little restaurant doesn't fit many diners, probably only 30 at the most. But it does have loyal customers. There are eclectic French novelties on display and even for sale. One of the most popular menu items is the pâté, which they sell by the pound for those who want to take some home. Another staple on the menu is the coq au vin. Flavorful and aromatic, this dish is not to be missed. French classics like chicken cordon bleu and beef bourguignon are on the menu as well. The French staff is cheerful and friendly. Closed Monday.

Cafe Gourmandises, 686 Peachtree Industrial Blvd., Ste. 200, Suwanee, GA 30024; (770) 945-6599; http://CafeGourmandises .com; French; $$$. One thing that the French are known for is their bread, and the bread at Cafe Gourmandises doesn't disappoint. Top that off with a fine-tuned chef using top-notch ingredients and are you are in for a stellar sandwich. Case in point is the authentic *croque madame,* served with tasty ham and Emmentaler cheese. Ask regulars, and each seems to have a favorite sandwich or dish, but all agree that the bread is phenomenal. They also serve escargot, quiches, and crepes, both savory and sweet. Don't miss out on the delicious macaroons for dessert. (Note: Restaurant closes early on most days, so it's certainly not the place for a late dinner. Check hours before visiting.) Closed Sunday.

Cafe Lily, 308 W. Ponce de Leon Ave., Ste. B, Decatur, GA 30030; (404) 371-9119; www.cafelily.com; Mediterranean; $$$. This Decatur neighborhood restaurant borrows its cuisine from many countries around the Mediterranean, including Italy, France, Greece, Spain, North Africa, and the Middle East. The menu has everything from Italian-style eggplant, to Spanish *tortas* with chorizo, to Greek souvlaki. At lunch try the PLP, which is a twist on the BLT: pancetta, lettuce, and tomato (*pomodoro*) served on a ciabatta roll. At dinner an appetizer of *pan de higo* or fig cake with manchego cheese and serrano ham is a nice start. For entrees try the *pinchitos,* Spanish lamb served with picante salsa verde. It also boasts a Wine Spectator Award for its comprehensive wine offering.

57th Fighter Group Restaurant, 3829 Clairmont Rd., Atlanta, GA 30341; (770) 234-0057; www.the57threstaurant.com; American; $$$. The 57th Fighter Group Restaurant has been an Atlanta institution since opening some 20 years ago. With its World War II theme, the main dining area of the restaurant has great views of the small DeKalb Peachtree Airport runways. The menu features American classics. Appetizer highlights include lobster risotto squares and firecracker calamari. Other menu highlights are the sage pork chop and 8-hour braised short ribs. Steaks and burgers are also available. There are private rooms and a patio area great for groups. Smaller tables lend themselves to more intimate dining but still allow views of the runways.

Kurt's Bistro, 3305 Peachtree Industrial Blvd., Duluth, GA 30096; (770) 623-4128; www.kurtsrestaurant.com; European; $$$. The previously German-only restaurant recently went through a slight change of menu to include more European dishes. Named after its owner, Kurt Eisele, who has been running the restaurant for over 25 years, the restaurant is dimly lit, perfect for a romantic date or a gathering of friends. European foods like Swiss fondue, escargot, frog's legs, and Bavarian pretzels are found on the appetizer menu. The meat-and-cheese plate is a smart way to get a sampling of the authentically European meats and cheeses. Of course, the pièce de résistance is the wiener schnitzel and spaetzle. The lightly breaded veal cutlet is served with a creamy spaetzle (pasta), and the addition of braised cabbage makes for a complete German experience. The meal is the perfect blend of flavors. For dessert, order the bananas Foster, a special dessert that staff prepares tableside. They also have a unique selection of brews, many of which won't be found elsewhere.

Zyka, 1677 Scott Blvd., Decatur, GA 30033; (404) 728-4444; www.zyka.com; Indian; $$. This long-standing Indian restaurant is tucked away among many car dealerships and stands next to a daycare center. Extremely hard to find, you need to be on the lookout for it. Unlike at many other Indian restaurants, you order at the counter and servers bring your food to the table. Chicken 65 and tandoori chicken are top-notch here. Vegetarians will enjoy the *aloo gobi* and the chana masala.

Sawicki's, 250 W. Ponce de Leon Ave., Decatur, GA 30030; (404) 377-0992; www.sawickisfoods.com; Sandwiches; $. Part meat shop, part market, and part sandwich shop, Sawicki's is high on flavor. You'll find high-end meats and cheeses, freshly made sandwiches, as well as condiments and some other grocery-store items here. But it is a specialty market, so expect pricier items than you would find at a regular supermarket. Notable sandwiches are the lamb, piled high with caramelized onions, and the veggie is unique with its hummus spread and salsa verde dressing. Also, the shrimp po'boy and the Italian, with a myriad of Italian meats and cheeses, are worth trying.

Southern Sweets Bakery, 186 Rio Circle, Decatur, GA 30030; (404) 373-8752; www.southernsweets.com; Desserts; $. Even if you've never eaten at the Southern Sweets Bakery, chances are you've eaten some of their desserts as they supply many of the restaurants in the surrounding area with their delicious treats. The small bakery is located not too far from the DeKalb Farmers' Market. The red velvet cake and apple pie are two of the best desserts available. They also offer completely vegan desserts and sandwiches. Though there are sandwiches, besides the chicken salad sandwich, the highlight of this establishment is the desserts.

Buford Highway

The Buford Highway area of Atlanta is where all our truly ethnic restaurants are found. Atlantans trek out to Buford Highway, located slightly north of the city, in search of the latest-and-greatest new find. All different ethnicities are represented along Buford Highway. Here you'll find Chinese, Korean, Mexican, and Vietnamese among others. As one would expect, the food is not only authentic but prices are low, as these establishments are not located in high-rent areas, and decor is kept to a minimum. It is not uncommon to have a fantastic and filling meal for under $10 here. Part of the fun of Buford Highway is getting out and exploring all there is to offer and knowing that you just might stumble on that next great restaurant.

 Foodie Faves

Bo Bo Garden, 5181 Buford Hwy., Atlanta, GA 30340; (678) 547-1881; Chinese; $$. If you are in need a Cantonese fix, Bo Bo

Garden will satisfy. Start off your meal with the three kinds of dumplings, which just happens to be a soup, even though it is listed in the appetizer section of the menu. If you are fan of duck tongue, you can find it here. The meat is fatty, and the Pepper Salt Duck Tongue at Bo Bo has a nice salty and crispy taste to it. For mains get the spare ribs and taro. They do take a while to make, but the dish is worth waiting for. Now for those who are used to a more Americanized version of Chinese food go for the clam and leeks. It is definitely representative of the cuisine and has traditional Chinese flavors. The fish-broth base is matched with ginger, garlic, onions, and carrots. Still, many love to visit for the lobster special, which is served up in snow pea leaves for just over $20. The staff is helpful, so don't be afraid to ask questions before ordering if you need clarification.

Canton House, 4825 Buford Hwy., Atlanta, GA 30341; (770) 936-9030; Dim Sum; $. For those in search of decent dim sum, you'll want to pay a visit to Canton House, although you can have a perfectly decent non-dim sum meal here as well. First, start your meal off with an order of their spring rolls. As far as dim sum, order the *siu mai*. Made with pork, shrimp, or chicken, they are all good, but pork is the best. Slather the chili sauce over top, and it is brilliant with the large pork pieces inside. Another hit is the steamed spare ribs, which are quite tasty, even though their appearance isn't the most appealing. Try to arrive by 11 a.m.; any time later than that you may be waiting for a table, as this is a very popular restaurant among the Atlanta Chinese population.

Chateau de Saigon, 4300 Buford Hwy., Ste. 218, Atlanta, GA 30345; (404) 929-0034; www.chateaudesaigon.com; Vietnamese; $. Upon entering, you'll notice that this establishment is a little nicer in look and decor than some of its other Buford Highway neighbors. Start your meal with the salt-and-pepper calamari and the papaya salad. You won't be disappointed. The calamari is tender with a light batter and is perfectly prepared. The shaking beef and the spicy lemongrass chicken are also fantastic entree options. You also have the option of ordering family-style, which is a great option if your party is a large group. This gives you the opportunity to try many dishes.

Chef Liu, 5221 Buford Hwy. Northeast, Atlanta, GA 30340; (770) 936-0532; Chinese; $. One of the menu highlights here is the lamb kebabs. If you are a lover of Shanghai juicy steamed pork buns, find them here, but be careful when eating as they contain soup inside, so they must be eaten whole in one bite. Many a customer's favorite is the leek pie, which is more like a pancake than a pie at all. If you are fan of duck, you don't want to miss it here as it is tender, but the skin is perfectly crispy. One last dish worth mentioning is the chicken meatballs hot pot. The tender meatballs are served with lots of mushrooms and tofu, and the light chicken broth is delicious. Definitely a solid choice for authentic dumplings and Chinese in the Atlanta area.

Com Vietnamese, 4005 Buford Hwy., Ste. E, Atlanta, GA 30345; (404) 320-0405; www.comgrillrestaurant.com; Vietnamese; $$. Com is perfect for those seeking non-pho Vietnamese food. When headed to Com, be on the lookout or you could easily miss it. It is near the corner of Clairmont Road and Buford Highway intersection. It's behind a gas station and is difficult to spot from the road. Start with the heavenly spring rolls, and don't stop there. Give the flat rice vermicelli with rice paper a try. Another great option is the duck-stuffed grape leaves. Probably the most popular dish here is the Com Special, a dish with rice, an egg, a shrimp-and-crab cake, and choice of meat. Waiters here speak excellent English, so there are no language barrier issues to be feared whatsoever. Their corkage fee is only $7, so feel free to bring a bottle of your choosing and enjoy.

El Norteño, 4929 Buford Hwy., Atlanta, GA 30341; (678) 209-4601; Mexican; $. Most of the customers here are Mexican, a good sign that this place is authentic. The salsa bar has 4 different kinds of salsas that vary in heat and spices. Note that this restaurant is all chicken; don't look for fish tacos or beef brisket. You can get a whole chicken, rice and beans, and soft corn tacos for under $20, enough to feed a family. I recommend getting the dark meat, as it is tender and juicy; the breast meat can be dry at times.

El Pastor, 5091 Buford Hwy. Northeast, Ste. D, Atlanta, GA 30340; (770) 451-4139; Mexican; $. Don't be put off by the strip mall location; the tacos here are very tasty. Stop by and order the namesake

El Pastor, a pork taco. Served in corn tortillas, as is authentically Mexican, the pork is sliced almost like brisket and it is mixed with diced onion and cilantro. Other kinds of tacos on the menu are: *borrego* (lamb), *bistec* (steak), *barbacoa* (fattier steak), and *lengua* (tongue). They also have sandwiches, or *tortas*. The Cuban and Hawaiian sandwiches are large, and the meat is tender and juicy. Warning: The place is really nothing to look at inside, and some may even be put off by the look of it, so if you are looking for pristine surroundings, you may want to go elsewhere.

Gu's Bistro, 5750 Buford Hwy., Ste. A, Doraville, GA 30340; (770) 451-8118; www.gusbistro.com; Chinese; $$. Gu's serves authentic Szechuan cuisine. The tea-smoked duck is a specialty of the restaurant, and if you are fan of duck, you don't want to miss out on this. The restaurant boasts an in-house smoker, and pork is smoked for several days. So if your server asks if you want your pork smoked or not, go for the smoked. One of the most popular dishes on the menu is the cumin lamb, which tends to be hot and spicy but still enjoyable. Others rave about the walnut shrimp, which is a good balance of mild if the other dishes ordered are spicy. Other menu highlights are the kung pao chicken and dan dan noodles. Tip: If you are not accustomed to the Chinese dishes that can be extremely peppery, then avoid the dishes on the menu marked with 3 peppers, which denote a very spicy meal.

Harmony Vegetarian, 4897 Buford Hwy., Ste. 109, Atlanta, GA 30341; (770) 457-7288 Vegetarian/Chinese; $. The name would lead one to believe this establishment only serves vegetarian food, which is true. However, they serve up many, many mock-meat entrees. They use imitation products to make entrees with beef-, pork-, and poultry-like flavors and textures. It is not only a haven for vegetarians, but some wonderful Chinese dishes are served here as well. Soups like hot-and-sour and wonton are extremely popular with vegetarians and omnivores alike. Mongolian beef and sesame chicken are very tasty here. Vegetarians and vegans will be pleased to be able to order from the entire menu and not just a small portion.

Lee's Bakery, 4005 Buford Hwy. Northeast, Atlanta, GA 30345; (404) 728-1008; Vietnamese; $. The pho is is solid. If you like banh mi, it is quite good here as well. They even have a combo of a half sandwich and order of pho for under $7, which is a phenomenal deal. The restaurant is extremely clean, and the ingredients are extremely high quality—sprouts, mint, cilantro, jalapeños—everything is fresh. Even if you are a pho fan or a banh mi fan exclusively, it's so worth it to get the combo. The banh mi with pork is tender, and the combination of crunchy vegetables and spicy jalapeños make bite after bite supremely delicious. For a drink, order the avocado smoothie or bubble tea.

Man Chung Hong, 5953 Buford Hwy. Northeast, Ste. 105, Atlanta, GA 30340; (770) 454-5640; Chinese/Korean; $$. Unusual, but this restaurant seems to be a mix of both Chinese and Korean. There's complimentary tea and kimchee. As the restaurant specializes in Szechuan dishes, the dry-fried eggplant and twice-cooked pork are particularly good. For the more authentic food, make sure to mention to your server that you prefer "regular" food and not the "Americanized" version. Skip the dumplings in favor of noodle dishes, which are tasty and have a great texture. Try the black bean noodles, also a good choice for vegetarians. Some guests even get to watch the noodles being made, which is way more impressive than watching pizza makers flip pizza dough. The restaurant does get very busy on Friday and Saturday night, so expect a wait at peak times. Tip: If you do have a large party, they do take reservations and are good about splitting checks.

Ming's Bar B Que, 5150 Buford Hwy. Northeast, # 300, Doraville, GA 30340; (770) 451-6985; Chinese; $. Walking by Ming's Bar B Que, you'll be lured in by the glistening and crispy-looking meats hanging on display in the window, reminiscent of some of the very Chinese restaurants that are located in New York City's Chinatown. Crispy duck and the barbecue are the real reasons to come here. Congee (a rice porridge) lovers will appreciate this dish here. The rice pairs well with the rich flavors of the meat it is served alongside.

Pho Dai Loi, 4186 Buford Hwy. Northeast, #G, Atlanta, GA 30345; (404) 633-2111; Vietnamese; $. The pho here is quite amazing as it is hearty with lots of meat, and the broth is extremely flavorful as well. If you are not a fan of pho, they also have vermicelli bowls or rice dinners. Food comes out quickly and service is prompt, so this could most certainly be a stop on your lunch hour. Note: They serve basil with your pho and not cilantro. Tip: While they do serve bubble tea, they don't carry the black pearls for it.

Pho 96, 5000 Buford Hwy., Ste. C, Atlanta, GA 30341; (770) 452-9644; Vietnamese; $. There are ton of Vietnamese restaurants along Buford Highway that serve pho. Pho 96 happens to look a little less sketchy from the outside than some of the other establishments. The staff is extremely friendly and helpful. There are also no problems with any sort of language barrier, as they speak fluent English. Order the *pho dac biet* (the pho with everything). It includes eye round steak, flank, marble brisket, soft tendon, and tripe. They also make great spring rolls and bubble tea.

Quoc Huong, 5150 Buford Hwy. Northeast, Atlanta, GA 30340; (770) 936-0605; Vietnamese; $. Quoc Huong serves up some of the best banh mi sandwiches in town. The *New York Times* agrees, as they wrote it up in an article detailing the best banh mi sandwiches in the country. That's probably due to a combination of the high-end, crispy French baguette it is served on, quality meat and veggies, as well as the light, slightly buttery mayo that makes this sandwich superb. The veggies used in the sandwich—cucumber, cilantro, jalapeños, pickled carrots, and daikon radish—really complement the meat, their crispiness in contrast to the tender meat. Tip: Buy 5 and get 1 free.

So Kong Dong, 5280 Buford Hwy. Northeast, #C, Atlanta, GA 30340; (678) 205-0555; Korean; $$. They make an excellent tofu soup here. There is a good mix of Koreans and non-Koreans to let you know that this is authentic and the real deal. Staff is here is friendly, and a majority of the servers do speak English well enough to provide good service. *Galbi* and bibimbap are stand out dishes. The *banchan* (side dishes served with the main meal) are plentiful.

Taqueria El Rey Del Taco, 5288 Buford Hwy. Northeast, Atlanta, GA 30340; (770) 986-0032; Mexican; $. The fun-loving restaurant is open 24 hours a day. You may want to brush up on your Spanish before going, as the majority of the menu is indecipherable to a non-Spanish speaker. However, some servers do speak English. If you are looking for unique meats like *lengua* (beef tongue), *cabeza* (beef cheek), and *buche* (pork stomach) to name a few, you will find them here. The corn tortillas are handmade and slightly charred for a pretty appearance. Start your meal off with their sensational guacamole. They are vegetarian-friendly as well, offering several non-meat tacos like mushroom and bean. Note that the tip is automatically added to the check.

Viet Tofu, 4897 Buford Hwy., Atlanta, GA 30341; (770) 458-9011; Vietnamese; $. This is not a sit-down restaurant but a buffet. Eggrolls, banh mi, and lemongrass chicken and stir-fried tofu are especially good here. They have a wall lined with a refrigerated section, so you can pop in and pick up meals or snacks to go. Note: There is no seating—takeout only.

Woo Nam Jeong Stone Bowl House Seoul Plaza, 5953 Buford Hwy., Ste. 107, Atlanta, GA 30340; (678) 530-0844; Korean; $$. The decor at Woo Nam Jeong Stone Bowl is a cut above the rest of the dining establishments in and along the Buford Highway Corridor. The dolsot bibimbap (stone soup) is wonderful and comparable to what can be found in New York City. These bowls come out extremely hot from the kitchen. They are so hot, in fact, that you can still hear a sizzle. If you prefer other items, the seafood pancake is quite tasty. They do have specials during the week, and especially at lunch, that are reasonably priced. In addition, there is also a multicourse tasting menu available that is upward of 12 courses, but the price is around $30. The chief cook, aka Grandma, is a very sweet old lady. She'll come out and greet large parties. At the end of a meal, she'll check with the patrons to make sure the meal met their expectations.

Hae Woon Dae, 5805 Buford Hwy. Northeast, Atlanta, GA 30340; (770) 451-7957; Korean BBQ; $$. While the prices for this Korean BBQ may be a little pricier than other options nearby, the quality is extremely high. Part of the difference in quality over other Korean BBQ joints in the city is that Hae Woon Dae's grills are charcoal, not gas grills. This difference seems to give the meat a smokiness that isn't found in other restaurants. They are open late night daily from 11 a.m. to 6 a.m. They close at midnight on Wednesday.

Havana Restaurant, 3979 Buford Hwy., Ste. 108, Atlanta, GA 30319; (404) 633-7549; www.havanarestaurantatlanta.com; Cuban; $. Cuban food fans were wholeheartedly disappointed when one of the most popular Cuban joints in Atlanta, Kool Korners, closed its doors. Thank goodness for Havana Restaurant, which has no doubt filled some of that void. This restaurant has now relocated to a nicer and newer building, which is a much-needed upgrade from its previous "hole in the wall" location. Portions here are huge. Two could easily split a sandwich entree, which comes with rice and beans. Plantains, yuca, and empanadas are all excellent here. Opt for chicken empanadas over pork. This restaurant gets quite crowded at lunch time. But for take-out orders, food is ready quickly. Note that they close at 6 p.m. on Sunday.

Little Szechuan, 5091 Buford Hwy. Northeast, Atlanta, GA 30340; (770) 451-0192; www.littleszechuanchefkongs.com; Chinese; $$

Many tout this as the best Chinese in the city. It does have some terrific entrees on its menu. For those who sometimes find traditional Chinese too salty or saucy, Little Szechuan would be a good choice because they do go light on the salt and sauce here. Portions are rather large. One entree can easily feed two. Vegetarian entrees can be found on the menu, but the better dishes are meat-oriented. Do be prepared for slow service. Note: The restaurant closes for lunch between 3 and 5 p.m. daily. Bring cash, as they accept credit cards but prefer not to take them as payment.

Panahar, 3375 Buford Hwy. Northeast, Ste. 1060, Atlanta, GA 30329; (404) 633-6655; www.panahar.com; Indian; $$. Although Bangladeshi cuisine is not very prominent in Atlanta, this is a fantastic representation of it. Chutneys are quite delicious (like the peach or spicy onion) and are great on of the many varieties of naan (bread) available. Garlic naan and onion naan are two of the best flavors, but even the plain naan is tasty. There are many vegetarian options, and a couple of standout dishes are *dharosh bhaaji* (sauteed okra with onion, tomatoes, and herbs) or the vegetable korma. One entree that is hands down a customer favorite is the chicken tikka; it should not be missed. One unique fact about this Bangladeshi restaurant is that the food is as flavorful as Indian, but not as hot and spicy. So, if you are a fan of Indian food but not the spice, rest assured you can visit Panahar and enjoy the fragrant cuisine without the heat. Also, you can BYOB with no corkage fees. Friday and Saturday get busy, so reservations are a must.

Sushi House Hayakawa, 5979 Buford Hwy., Ste. A-10, Atlanta, GA 30340; (770) 986-0010; www.atlantasushibar.com; Sushi; $$$. Although it is one of the more expensive Buford Highway restaurants, this is the real deal. Some sushi restaurants try to be chic by having a trendy decor or loud dance music, but that's not what you'll find at Sushi House Hayakawa. The chef really is well trained and knows his stuff. That is why most choose the *omakase,* or chef's choice, instead of ordering on their own. Regulars like to sit at the sushi bar and converse with the chef and watch as he prepares their sushi. For those who aren't sushi fans, the noodle bowls are quite good, too. Good selection of sake. Reservations are a must on Friday and Saturday. Closed Monday.

Specialty Stores & Markets

Fil-Am Star Cafe and Bakery, 5150 Buford Hwy. Northeast, Ste. A-170, Doraville, GA 30340; (678) 381-1524; www.filamstarcafe .com; Filipino; $. This is a relatively new restaurant in the Buford Highway scene. It adds to the culinary diversity, as there aren't many Filipino restaurants in Atlanta. The restaurant is rather small, with only 7 or 8 tables and counter seating. Food is served family-style, so it's best to bring a group of friends. Start your meal off with the *lumpia* (fried spring rolls) or the *siopao* (steamed buns filled with your choice of chicken, pork, sausage, or beef). The top dishes to be found here are the fried whole tilapia, the *menudo* (cubed pork and tomato sauce), and the adobo (a stew made with soy and vinegar). Be sure to check their Facebook page, as some menu items are not always available, and they update their menu here daily.

Cobb & Northwest Atlanta (Marietta, Smyrna, Vinings, Woodstock, Kennesaw, Acworth)

Cobb County and its outlying areas have been a large part of the urban sprawl Atlanta has experienced over the last 10 to 15 years. One of the most famous landmarks in all of the state of Georgia is the Big Chicken, part of the outside decor of a KFC restaurant in

Marietta. What makes this KFC unique is the 56-foot-tall chicken that is part of the restaurant. Many locals like to give directions with this as a starting point. An uproar was created when KFC wanted to tear down the structure in 1993 after storms had damaged it. So many people complained that the company repaired it, and it remains an extremely popular landmark in this Atlanta suburb. This part of the Atlanta metro area is home to many families. With lots of affordable housing and a great school system, most restaurants are geared toward families. Fact: Actress Julia Roberts hails from Smyrna.

Foodie Faves

Atlanta Cheesecake Company, 1300 Shiloh Rd., Kennesaw, GA 30144; (770) 427-4896; www.atlantacheesecakecompany.com; Sandwiches/Desserts; $. An interesting concept, this establishment offers not only fresh-made cheesecakes, but high-quality sandwiches, teas, and specialty desserts and custom cakes. Three siblings started the Atlanta Cheesecake Company in 1988 in Anniston, Alabama. This was all based on their grandmother's cheesecake recipe. Cheesecakes can be ordered from the website to be delivered anywhere in the United States. With the need for more space and a more metropolitan area, they relocated to Atlanta and have been in their Kennesaw space for several years now. The restaurant falls into the fast casual arena. Items are made on-site and can be picked up and taken away or eaten on-site in the beautiful atmosphere. Many of the high-end wood furnishings were custom-made for the restaurant. There's also free Wi-Fi for those want to linger. Sandwiches like tuna salad, chicken salad, and pimiento cheese are on the menu. Highlights are the roast beef salad, Hawaiian ham, and deviled egg. Roast beef salad sandwich sounds weird, but it is delicious. And there was something special mixed in (nutmeg?) that gave it that extra oomph. The Hawaiian ham was perfection with actual small pieces of pineapple mixed in with the cheese and mayo. Sides offered are fruit cup (mixed with blueberries, strawberries, and cantaloupe), coleslaw (light on the mayo—thumbs up), and mashed potato salad (good flavor with bits of egg mixed in as well). However, they do carry chips as well. Extra: They also make custom-order cakes for weddings and special events.

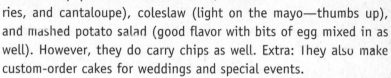

Big Chow Grill, 1 Galleria Pkwy., Ste. 1B1, Atlanta, GA 30339; (770) 405-2464; Asian; $$. Big Chow Grill (formerly the Real Chow, Baby), is a restaurant where you choose the ingredients you like and then let the staff cook them for you. But it is not like a fondue; this is more like stir-fry. You pick your meat, vegetables, starch (rice, noodles, etc.), and they cook them up for you in a seasoning of your choosing. Those who have food allergies have the option of having their food cooked separately. What's nice about this is that with the variety of offerings in each category, it is possible to go many times and never have the same meal twice. The best option is to choose unlimited trips for around $13. This allows you to pick 2 or 3 small bowls and try different things, versus trying to mix all the ingredients into one bowl. This is a very popular spot for families, so those who want a quiet spot with no kids around, go elsewhere. Tip: Great sweet tea.

Big Pie in the Sky Pizzeria, 2090 Baker Rd., Ste. A103, Kennesaw, GA 30144; (770) 420-8883; Pizza; $. The tagline for Big Pie in the Sky is "Slices as Big as Your Head." That is not an exaggeration. The restaurant was made forever famous by the television show *Man v. Food,* where host Adam Richman and another guest tried to eat one of their huge pizzas in under an hour. Contest rules are simple: If you and a friend can devour their meat pizza—which comes piled high with 5 different meats—in under 1 hour you win $250. Of course, most people are filled up after one slice of pizza. There's no table service at Big Pie in the Sky. Guests place their order at the counter, and food is brought out to your table. Besides pizza, they also offer subs and salads, but the highlight here is, obviously, pizza. The big kahuna with toppings of ham, bacon, feta cheese, and pineapple is quite tasty and worth a try for those who enjoy Hawaiian pizza. Of course, the "carnivore special" with 5 different meats is also a hit. No matter what kind of pizza you order, rest assured that the toppings will be plentiful. (Note: During lunch hours, they offer a special of a slice of pizza with 2 toppings and a drink for $5. Their specialty slices are about the same price and provide more toppings and are a better value.)

Crepe Revolution, 4600 W. Village Place, Smyrna, GA 30080; (770) 485-7440; www.creperevolution.com; Crepes; $$. If you think that crepes are only for dinner, think again. Crepe Revolution offers crepes for brunch, lunch, and dinner. What is also surprising is how upscale and somewhat swanky the decor is. Expect dark woods, warm colors, and a beautiful separate bar area. This is terrific place for a group outing. Customers have a choice of building their own crepe by choosing their own ingredients down to the type of crepe, seasoning, and sauce. Some of the best crepes are the chipotle pork with tender juicy pork and roasted chipotles, covered in a spicy chipotle sauce, and the duck confit crepe. This crepe comes with portobello mushrooms, spinach, shallots, and almonds in a port wine reduction sauce and is consistently a customer favorite. No visit would be complete without a dessert crepe: Get the bananas Foster crepe. The rich sauce oozes out of the crepe, and just a bit of crepe, a banana slice, and some sauce makes for the perfect bite. It is worth a trip to Crepe Revolution just for that dessert alone. A final nice touch is the French press coffee served in its own individual pot to each guest.

Cuban Diner, 1484 Roswell Rd., Marietta, GA 30062; (770) 509-2576; www.mariettacubandiner.com; Cuban; $$. Located not too far from the Big Chicken in Marietta, the Cuban Diner is small restaurant run by a Cuban husband-and-wife team. The decor is made lively with Cuban artwork and pictures. The enthusiasm from the team here is contagious. You feel at home right away. Starters like chicken or beef empanadas should not be missed. Anyone who is a fan of pork tamales won't want to miss these either. Served atop corn husks, they are extremely flavorful. Of course the ever-popular Cuban sandwich is served up with ham, pork, swiss, mustard, mayo, and pickles on Cuban bread, and it's delicious. But even better is the *media noche* sandwich. This is the same as the Cuban, but served on slightly sweet bread and quite flavorful. For something other than a sandwich, choose the light but tasty *pescado a la plancha*. Perfectly prepared, it is served with a Cuban lime marinade and grilled onions. Lunch is terrific deal offering a sandwich or entree with 2 sides topping out at under $10. Notable sides are the *maduros* (sweet plantains), yuca fries, or beans and rice. At dinner try the *ropa vieja,* a shredded beef brisket in a tomato sauce, or the *lechon asado,* a traditional Cuban dish of stir-fried pork; both are standouts. The beer and wine list is small here. Instead opt for authentic drinks like the milk shakes of mamey, mango, or papaya. Note: They are closed Sunday.

Dogwood Terrace, 4975 N. Main St., Acworth, GA 30101; (770) 627-4069; www.dogwoodterraceacworth.com; American; $$$. Dogwood Terrace, located in historic Acworth, is not only a restaurant but a special events facility. It is beautifully decorated and contains wood and materials mostly sourced from different cities in Georgia. Lunch consists mostly of salads, wraps, sandwiches, and pizzas. For dinner, there are plenty of seafood starters for those who enjoy them. Crab cakes with lemon caper butter are tasty, as is the sesame ahi tuna and the lobster quesadilla. But don't miss the artichoke dip spiked with Sriracha sauce or the house-made potato chips with blue cheese sauce and balsamic reduction. Skip the gourmet pizzas in favor of more substantial mains like the White Marble Farms pork tenderloin marinated in garlic, cumin, and cayenne pepper and served up with a spicy apple chutney, or the crispy duck topped with a sweet-and-sour apricot sauce. On Sunday only the brunch is offered from 10 a.m. until 2 p.m. The nice thing is that while a buffet is offered, customers can also order from a regular a la carte menu, including items like crab Benedict or breakfast burrito. The restaurant is closed on Monday and for dinner on Sunday.

Douceur de France, 367 Glover St. Southeast, Marietta, GA 30060; (770) 425-5050; www.douceurdefrance.com; Bakery; $. Located between some railroad tracks and what seems to be a junkyard, you wouldn't find Douceur de France unless you were looking for it. The converted house is quite cozy inside. The gravel parking lot isn't huge, and the place can get very crowded during peak lunch hours. While the location is extremely odd for a French bakery, the goods are extremely tasty and fresh. Word is that the owners believe in making everything fresh and from scratch, and the baking starts early each day. There's usually a handful of French nationals in the restaurant at any given time, which attests to the authenticity of the goods. The quiche lorraine is delicious. Although they have various breakfast items and sandwiches, it is the desserts and pastries that are the highlights at this authentic French bakery. Don't miss the almond croissants or macaroons. Tip: If you like to bake, buy your butter here and you won't regret it. Bakery is closed on Sunday. Open Mon through Sat from 7:30 a.m. until 6 p.m.

Elevation Chop House, 1723 McCollum Pkwy., Bldg. 600, Kennesaw, GA 30144; (770) 485-7469; www.elevationchophouse .com; American; $$. This restaurant is only a few years old. While many chain restaurants line the Kennesaw neighborhood, this is a welcome respite from them. The restaurant specializes in wood-grilled steaks and seafood. There's live music on the weekends, and you can even enjoy a biplane ride before dinner.

Harry's Pizza and Subs, 2150 Powers Ferry Rd. Southeast, Atlanta, GA 30339; (770) 955-4413; www.harryspizzaandsubs.com; Pizza; $. Harry's Pizza offers a New York–style pizza that seems to be in a '80s time warp (in a good way). This is the type of pizza that comes near perfectly done in every way—you don't even have to wipe off any excess grease. Crust is done just right, and you'll eat the entire piece, even the crust. The Greek salad with its creamy dressing is divine and a perfect balance to the carb-heavy pizza. While whole pies can be ordered, you are better off stopping in at lunch and ordering a slice or two. The '80s decor is complete with classic video games like Pac-Man. Harry passed on several years ago, but his family keeps running the place, and service is friendly, albeit often slow. It is centrally located to two major interstates, I-75 and I-285. Many business travelers staying in close proximity to this pizza joint opt to get their food delivered. They offer a limited delivery area with a $10 minimum order.

Hot Dog Heaven, 8558 Main St., Woodstock, GA 30188; (770) 591-5605; Hot Dogs; $. This is a little restaurant located in the downtown Woodstock area. Although there is not much seating, the service is quick and efficient. Visit at off-peak times to be guaranteed seating. The owner provides very friendly service. Visit a few times and she'll get to know your name, and you'll be like family. Not only do they serve hot dogs, but they also have some very tasty corn dogs, and the burgers here are delicious, too. Hot dogs on poppy seed buns are extra delicious. Note: They only accept cash here. Rumor: If the Coke delivery person comes in and sees you drinking a Coke product, he will buy your lunch.

Izba Crepes, 3000 Windy Hill Rd. Southeast, Ste. 132, Marietta, GA 30067; (678) 402-5574; www.izbacrepes.com; Crepes; $. In comparison to **Crepe Revolution** (p. 149), also in Cobb County, Izba is a little more casual in its decor, and the choices, while tasty, are a little less imaginative. Izba does a good catering business as well as selling crepes from their restaurant. Two of the standouts on the menu are the Philly cheesesteak and the Mexican crepe. There are a few vegetarian crepe options as well. Of course, the build-your-own-crepe option is also available.

Ji Boute Cajun Cafe, 800 Whitlock Ave., Ste. 103, Marietta, GA 30064; (770) 794-0779; Cajun; $$. It isn't a fancy place to grab a bite to eat, but what Ji Boute Cajun Cafe lacks in decor, it makes up for in food quality. In true Cajun fashion, there's chicken-and-sausage gumbo as well as sausage red beans with rice. Both are quite tasty, but the gumbo tends to be a tad better. The service can be hit or miss. Sometimes staff is very helpful and friendly, and at other times, less on top of things. Overall, it is a solid spot for decent Cajun food in the area.

Kiosco—A Taste of Colombia, 48 Powder Springs Rd., Marietta, GA 30060; (678) 337-7999; www.kioscocolombianrestaurant.com; Latin; $$. This small restaurant (only about 7 small tables are on the inside) is located along the outskirts of the Marietta Square, a popular destination for families, especially with live bands and festivals on the weekends. It is one of the anchor restaurants of the **Taste of Marietta Festival** (see p. xxi) each year. The restaurant makes their two most popular menu items: authentic empanadas and tamales. The crispy empanadas are filled with tender and tasty beef or chicken, and their huge tamales come wrapped in a corn husk. The tender pork inside mixes well with the spicy habañero sauce poured atop it. Dining in the restaurant, patrons can explore the more complex dishes as well. The *carne* *con patacones,* a shredded beef entree with plantains, is a dish full of flavor, and for a lighter portion, the salmon with mango sauce is quite delicious and a nice departure from the meat-centric dishes. At lunch, prices are under $9. Dishes come with a choice of soup or bean salad. Note: Lunch is served Mon through Sat from 11 a.m. to 3 p.m. Best bet for a quick meal without a wait is to come during lunch on Saturday or dinner weekdays.

Minato Japanese, 2697 Spring Rd., Atlanta, GA 30006; (770) 432-6012; Japanese/Sushi; $$. A favorite of locals and out-of-towners, Minato serves up some truly excellent sushi. A little bit different from other sushi restaurants in the Atlanta area, the focus here is on the food, not trendy and upscale decor. The staff is very friendly and goes above and beyond to make sure diners are pleased with the food and service. Nigiri is not only fresh, but the amount of fish is generous. Start with the dumplings and the squid salad. Some of the best menu items are the super crunch roll and the spicy maguro. It can be difficult to find the restaurant, as it is a little off the beaten path; it is located behind a Papa John's pizza. If you have a GPS, use it to locate the restaurant. (Tip: Ask for the Cowboy Hat. It isn't on the menu, but ask for it; you will be in for a nice treat. It is a scallop served on top of a rice cracker with crab salad.)

Motherland Kitchen and Spices, 2359 Windy Hill Rd., Ste. 340, Marietta, GA 30067; (770) 402-7077; www.motherlandkitchen.com; African; $$. Motherland Kitchen and Spices combines a variety of ethnic cuisines: African, soul, Caribbean, and Nigerian food are all represented. Owner Sabina has created a unique establishment you won't find anywhere else. Menu highlights are the curry or jerk chicken, and goat or oxtail stew. For something unique try the peanut-butter stew with leeks, tomatoes, and a choice of chicken or beef, or the fried hot-peppered snails. The soups here are hearty and consist of fish and several proteins. There's also special consideration given to diabetics and vegetarians with a decent selection of menu items. The restaurant is open each day and does a good amount of business, and they also have catering services available. And if you'd like to try cooking this cuisine at home, pick up some of the spices and seasonings available for purchase at their restaurant or online. These specialty spices are imported directly from African countries. All spices and seasonings are available for under $5.

Mountain Biscuits, 1718 Old Hwy. 41, Marietta, GA 30060; (770) 419-3311; Breakfast; $. Located near the National Historic Site, Kennesaw Mountain National Battlefield, Mountain Biscuits is a popular stop for families on their way to or from visiting the mountain. The establishment itself is a rather small space, but with its bright yellow color, it has a charming, country appeal. The interior has a few tables for seating, and there is also an attached gravel parking lot, but it doesn't accommodate a lot of cars. It can get quite busy on weekend mornings when patrons flock there for a hearty breakfast biscuit. The biscuits here are huge, soft, and fluffy, but are substantial enough that they don't fall apart after a couple bites, as can be the case sometimes. The meat inside the biscuits is quality, and the flavor comes through even though the biscuits are quite large. Highlights are the bacon, egg, and cheese biscuit; sausage biscuit; and the chicken biscuits. The restaurant is open for lunch as well, but the highlight is the breakfast biscuit, obviously, since that is what the restaurant is named after. Breakfast is served all day from 6 a.m. to 2 p.m., and lunch is served from 11 a.m. to 2 p.m. Closed Sunday.

Mulberry Street Pizza, 4355 Cobb Pkwy. Southeast, Atlanta, GA 30339; (770) 988-8646; www.mulberrystreetpizza.com; Pizza; $. This pizza joint was started by several past employees of Little Italy Pizza, a very popular pizza restaurant located in Athens, Georgia. About 1 to 1.5 hours outside the city of Atlanta, Athens is home to the University of Georgia. You'll see the nod to UGA in the decor of Mulberry Street, with UGA memorabilia throughout the restaurant. When they opened up, they installed new ovens that reach a temperature of over 500 degrees, which results in a nice char. The ratio of sauce, cheese, and toppings produces a quality pizza, which is sold by the slice as well as the pie. In addition to pizza, the restaurant also serves a killer lasagna. Don't miss adding a salad to your pizza or meal, as the salads are quite substantial and have quality ingredients. Try the Greek salad with feta cheese, artichoke hearts, and banana peppers. They offer a lunch special of 2 slices of pizza with 1 topping each plus a drink for under $6.

Olive Bistro, 3230 Cobb Pkwy., Atlanta, GA 30339; (770) 272-8900; www.olivebistro.com; Mediterranean; $$. Although the restaurant is located in strip mall, it shouldn't deter anyone from visiting, as the Mediterranean food served here is top-notch. Although it is small inside with only about 10 or 11 tables, it makes for a cozy atmosphere. During the evening, when the lights are turned down, it even has a romantic feel to it. Don't miss out on the hummus or the falafel. The local paper recently rated their falafel as the best in the city. It is outstanding with a crisp outside and soft and moist inside. For a sampling of the best items order the Mediterranean platter, which comes with a choice of 4 of the following: falafel, hummus, baba ghanoush, tabbouleh, eggplant, Tuscan beans, or Greek salad. Servers here are attentive and enthusiastic about the food. Can get crowded during peak lunch hours.

Oyster Cafe, 3060 Cobb Pkwy. Northwest, Ste. 101, Kennesaw, GA 30152; (770) 529-2197; Seafood; $$. Open for over 25 years in Kennesaw, the previous location was more a small shack than a cafe, but since moving to a much larger space, the restaurant is better able to accommodate its customers. As the name suggests, oysters are the star of the show here. They are available in the typical fashion—steamed or on the half shell. But regulars know to order the oyster special. This comes with butter, garlic, cheese, lemon, and paprika. They are baked and so tasty that you won't want to share with other dining companions. At lunch, order the fried shrimp sandwich. The dinner selection is much better. Opt for the buffalo shrimp or catfish filets. If you can't decide, go for the combination platter that offers a half dozen mix and match of shrimp, scallops, or oysters with a choice of perch, tilapia, or catfish. The beer and wine selection is rather limited, with mostly domestics on draft.

Peace, Love and Pizza, 4200 Wade Green Rd., Kennesaw, GA 30144; (770) 792-8989; www.peaceloveandpizza.com; Pizza; $$. This a joint venture between brothers Dave and Richie DeSantis, who have been involved in the restaurant industry one way or another most of their lives. The brothers exude a genuine pride in their restaurant and enthusiasm about what they are doing, which has resulted in a loyal following. Note that the restaurant is a take-out rather than sit-down restaurant. There are a few tables outside and only one inside. They offer 3 pizza sizes—a 10-inch, a 14-inch, and 18-inch. The 10-inch has 4 slices and is adequate for one person. The 14-inch is 8 slices, and the 18-inch has 12 slices. The ingredients are very fresh, and the mozzarella, pepperoni, and sausage are excellent on the traditional pizza. One of the things that set this pizza place apart, besides the toppings, are the various pizza sauces. Besides a traditional red sauce, ricotta sauce, or olive oil, they offer spicy roasted red pepper and barbecue sauces. For something unique to the restaurant, order the Desperado pizza, but only if you like it spicy. This pizza comes with hot peppers and hot sauce along with chicken, bacon, and pineapple. Another standout pizza is the Demon's Spicy White Love, which comes with ricotta sauce, spinach, garlic, roasted red peppers, chicken, and hot chili sauce. Peace, Love and Pizza also offers a variety of 8 salads and 10 different sandwiches as well. Menu items have comical names, such as the I Wanna Hold Your Ham sub and the Groovylicious pizza. In addition to the Caesar, Greek, and Caprese salads, the Frou Frou Salad is a highlight with sunflower seeds, spinach, pineapple, and artichoke hearts. Note: Their website is set up to take online orders, where pizzas are highly customizable. Owners are very much in favor of being environmentally friendly and recycle most trash.

Pho Huang Long, 331 Pat Mell Rd. Southeast, Marietta, GA 30060; (770) 384-0530; Vietnamese; $. This is a great ethnic find for those in the Marietta/Cobb area seeking authentic Vietnamese. The restaurant is relatively small with only about 10 tables. Service is quick and efficient despite the fact that there is usually only one waitress who doubles as the cashier. The pho (Vietnamese noodle soup) here is splendid. Very authentic, it comes with tripe and is served with the meat still pink, which cooks through as it sits in the broth. Of course, the accompaniments to this soup—cilantro, jalapeños, sprouts, and basil—are all extremely fresh. Most of the customers are Vietnamese, which speaks to the authenticity of the restaurant. With an ethnic store attached to the restaurant, it is worth perusing the goods after you are done eating.

Presto Latin Restaurant Bakery, 1157 Roswell Rd., Marietta, GA 30062; (770) 973-1280; www.prestorestaurant.com; Latin; $. Although the decor may be bare bones, Presto has one of the best lunch deals found in Cobb County. It does have a regular lunch menu, but their lunch specials are such a great deal, it is best to take advantage of them. Start your meal off with an order of empanadas, but be careful to go easy on the hot green sauce that accompanies them. Depending on the server, non-Spanish-speaking customers may experience a bit of language barrier if they aren't familiar with Latin/South American food. Note that entrees come with a choice of soup and potatoes (regular or sweet plantains). The whole fried-fish option is a filling lunch special, although be prepared to do a little work to get to the meat of the dish around all the bones. If you want to get a true sampling of Colombian food, order the *bandeja paisa*. At $11.50, it is well worth its price. The huge plate consists of a chorizo link, grilled beef, fried pork skin, fried sweet plantains, a corn cake, red beans and rice, an avocado half, and a fried egg. Tip: There's a smaller version called *paisita* for about half the cost. They also have unique fruit drinks that complement the food quite well. Think mango, papaya, and other tropical flavors. They are offered mixed with your choice of water or milk. A favorite is the *guayaba* (guava), sweet but not too sweet, and very refreshing on a hot summer day.

Siam Square, 1995 Windy Hill Rd. Southeast, Smyrna, GA 30080; (770) 333-1700; www.siamsquarethaicuisine.com; Thai; $$$. This Thai spot is another one of those stellar restaurants located in an unassuming strip mall. Once inside, the strip mall location will be forgotten as the stained concrete floor and upscale Asian decor create a beautiful ambience. Candlelit tables make for a romantic evening at Siam Square, but it also works for groups, too. Your server will bring you a glass of refreshing cucumber water to start your meal. Unless you really want a glass of wine, I'd stick with the water, especially if plans are to order something with heat. Start with basil rolls and winter rolls. (Winter rolls are fried basil rolls.) The sauce for the winter rolls was sweeter than that for the regular basil rolls. The winter rolls are definitely a standout among the appetizers. At lunch the drunken noodles and spicy chicken are good choices. Also note that this a good lunchtime choice if you need to be in and out quickly. For entrees the peppery green curry catfish and the Massaman curry with beef are some of the best choices. Especially for sharing, this is a great combo; one is hot and the other is pretty mild. The catfish, chock-full of catfish nuggets, bell peppers, and eggplant, is absolutely delicious. The lightly fried basil leaves also added yet another dimension of flavor and quality to the dish. The beef Massaman had a great flavor combination that runs circles around almost any other Massaman curry at many other Thai restaurants in the city. Closed for lunch on Saturday and Sunday.

Simpatico, 25 N. Park Sq. Northeast, Marietta, GA 30060; (770) 792-9086; www.willieraes.net/Simpatico.html; American/ Mediterranean/Tapas; $$$. Simpatico, opened in 2001, is located at the corner of the historic Marietta Square. Their sister restaurant,

Willie Rae's (p. 168), is the Cajun counterpart, and you can order off either menu regardless of which restaurant you are seated in. It is difficult to pin down this restaurant to a certain cuisine. There's Italian, Thai, and Southwest influences on the menu. So it's certainly a good option for a group in which each person likes something different. The fresh oysters—curry-crusted with lemongrass cream—are unique and worth trying when they are in season. For mains, seafood seems to be more of a standout than meat-centric meals. Try the bacon-wrapped shrimp over saffron risotto, or the shrimp and orzo served in goat cheese cream sauce with olives, basil, and sun-dried tomatoes. Skip dessert and head to one of the nearby bakeries or dessert spots to end the meal. The restaurant is only open for dinner; closed Sunday and Monday.

Soba Bistro and Bar, 1060 E. Piedmont Rd., Marietta, GA 30062; (770) 971-1888; www.sobabistro.com; Chinese/Sushi; $$$. Soba's cuisine is Asian—with an offering of sushi and Chinese. The decor is nicely done and very upscale. Menu highlights are the firecracker shrimp and the tuna steak. Portions are large and the quality is top-notch, too. Save room for the *xango* cheesecake. This is cheesecake wrapped in a wonton-like substance and drizzled with lemon, raspberry, and chocolate sauces. The plating of everything is absolutely beautiful. Great care is taken in not only the food preparation but the presentation as well. Servers are helpful, friendly, and efficient, making great recommendations based on customer preferences.

Starlight Cafe, 166 Roswell St. Northeast, Marietta, GA 30060; (678) 831-0709; American; $. Only open since 2010, this breakfast- and lunch-only spot has garnered many fans in its brief existence. Serving salads, sandwiches, salads, burgers, and hot dogs, the last two remain the most popular. The burgers come as half-pound standards, but diners have the option of ordering only a quarter pound. There are over 10 different kinds of burgers; with names like the Flyin' Hawaiian, Cowboy Melt, Three Alarm, and Heart Attack, it is obvious these are not dainty in any way. The hot dogs are nothing to sneeze at, either. The quarter-pound dogs are available grilled, steamed, or even fried. Their names are no less bizarre: Reuben dog or Kansas City dog are 2 available. All burgers, sandwiches, and dogs come as a combo with choice of 1 side and a drink. The usual suspects of fries, onion rings, slaw, and mac 'n' cheese are available, but for something out of the ordinary go for the fried cassava chips. Note: They are only open Mon through Fri from 10 a.m. to 2 p.m., and Sat until 3 p.m.

Tassa Roti Shop, 224 Powers Ferry Rd., Marietta, GA 30067; (770) 977-3163; http://tassarotishop.com; Caribbean; $. Tassa Roti Shop is a small restaurant located along Powers Ferry Road in Marietta. The term "restaurant" is used very loosely, as this is a small house that has been converted into a restaurant. There are about 10 tables set up in the bare-bones, renovated house, but when the weather allows, guests want to be seated on the small deck outside. The owners are welcoming to all, and if they find out it is your first time, they are more than happy to explain different items on the buffet. These include—chicken (jerk, stew, and curry), curried potatoes, callaloo (spinach-like with okra and onions), slaw, and rice and beans. It wouldn't be a Caribbean restaurant without roti. This bread of sorts is very similar to Indian naan. It is round, soft, and fluffy, which is perfect for sopping up the spicy curry sauce. You can also stuff the meat and sauce inside and eat it like a wrap. Although the restaurant setup and serving gear are a bit rustic (the roti is located in a cooler next to the buffet), the food is quite tasty. Adventurous eaters should sample the condiments located just above the buffet. The red pepper is extremely hot, and the achar is a less-spicy condiment made with mango or sometimes with lime. There is a menu to order from, but no one bothers with that, at least not at lunch time. Try a traditional drink, mauby, if they have it. It is not very sweet but has a great flavor. For something more sweet, try the kola champagne, a nonalcoholic soft drink.

Tomo, 3256 Cobb Pkwy., Atlanta, GA 30339; (770) 690-0555; www.tomorestaurant.com; Japanese; $$$. Run by Chef Tom Naito, a native of Japan who came to the United States to study and has worked in New York, Boston, and even in Las Vegas at the prestigious Nobu Restaurant. After learning from Master Chef Nobu

Matsuhisa, Tom has began his own style at Tomo. He mixes his training in the art of French and Italian cooking with Japanese offerings. The presentation of dishes is like a work of art. The fresh and seasonal fish flown in from Japan keeps customers coming back. Prices for lunch are very reasonable. For lunch order the bento box with the chef's choice sushi. This includes miso soup, 2 types of salad (one with ginger dressing, the other a seaweed salad), brown noodles, 4 California rolls, and 4 pieces of nigiri. At dinner start with the *hamachi* (yellowtail) sashimi or the *usuzukuri* (fluke sashimi), which comes with cilantro and Sriracha sauce. Staff is adept at making recommendations and steering those who are unsure of what to order in the right direction. Don't skip dessert either, as this place does much better than just a bowl of green tea ice cream. Order the mango sunny-side up if it is available. It consists of coconut panna cotta and mango jelly. Artfully presented and extremely delicious, it is a decadent end to a stellar meal. Reservations recommended. Closed Monday.

Udipi Cafe, 2772 Cumberland Blvd., Smyrna, GA 30080; (770) 404-6263; www.udipicafegeorgia.com; Indian; $. This vegetarian Indian restaurant is popular for office workers in the area during lunch. The decor is pretty upscale and not at all what one would expect from a strip mall location. While the menu has many options, they are strictly South Indian vegetarian. So while a vegetarian would feel quite comfortable here, carnivorous folks may feel like they are missing something. However, it is unlikely with the tasty buffet options and the delicious *thalis* offered. *Thalis* are combination plates that offer 6 or 7 vegetarian dishes with a large order of basmati rice in the center and some sort of naan. These dishes could include chana masala, dal, pickles, *rasam,* raita, or a variety of other choices. For those unfamiliar with Indian food, this is a terrific introduction, and much of the food will not be peppery. All of this is under $10 at lunch. Order off the regular menu at dinner for a variety of Indian specialties.

Umezono, 2086 Cobb Pkwy. Southeast, Ste. B, Smyrna, GA 30080; (770) 933-8808; www.umezono.us; Japanese; $$. Pay no attention to the fact that this restaurant is located next door to a gentlemen's club. This restaurant is not fancy, but it is a fantastic establishment to have an exceptional lunch (Monday through Friday only). Most lunch offerings come with a starter of miso soup and salad with ginger dressing. Then choose from several options like fried shrimp, pork *katsu,* or choices of sushi rolls. You'll leave completely satisfied whether your preference is for cooked or uncooked food. At dinner, give the more-extensive menu a try, which includes sushi, noodle, and teriyaki dishes.

Vingenzo's Woodstock, 105 E. Main St., Ste. 100, Woodstock, GA 30188; (770) 924-9133; www.vingenzos.com; Italian; $$. Some of the best pasta and Neapolitan pizza can be found in this unassuming downtown Woodstock restaurant. Owner Michael is meticulous and insistent that every detail about his Italian eatery be perfect. However, this doesn't get in the way of his charming and charismatic personality shining through. Almost all ingredients, including water, are imported from Italy. There's a pasta machine, which cranks out 3 house-made pastas each day. Even the mozzarella is made in-house. Start the meal with the grandioso tasting, which comes with 3 different styles of mozzarella, a small salad with a balsamic reduction, and a choice of 2 or 3 types of meat to add to the selection for good measure. The quality ingredients used are evident in the pizza as well. La Margherita, although simple, was bursting with flavor, as was the spicy sopressata with fennel salami and Taggiasche black olives. Try at least one pizza when visiting. As for pastas, old favorites like *frutti di mare* and *al olio* can be found on here. But the gnocchi al forno (with house-made sausage and fresh ricotta) shouldn't be missed. Probably the most unusual pasta and a house specialty is the *sugo di domenica*. This is a rich tomato sauce complemented by tasty shreds of pork. Simply outstanding. Even desserts are made on-site. In hot summer months indulge in the gelato. The ricotta cheesecake is a rich and creamy alternative with its Marsala-soaked raisins. Wines are carefully chosen, yet very affordable with all glasses under $8.

Willie Rae's, 25 N. Park Sq. Northeast, Marietta, GA 30060; (770) 792-9086; Cajun; $$. Located next door to their sister restaurant, **Simpatico** (p. 162), Willie Rae's is the more casual and less expensive of the two eateries. Start a meal with the crawfish tails, half a pound, cornmeal-battered, fried, and served up with a spicy remoulade, they are a great value. The mussels are another good pick, and spicy as well, cooked in a chipotle broth. Fish tacos with cilantro/jalapeño tartar sauce are tasty, as are the po'boys (choice of oysters, shrimp, or crawfish). For a mix of Cajun and Southern, try the shrimp and grits.

Yakitori Jinbi, 2421 Cobb Pkwy. Southeast, Smyrna, GA 30080; (770) 818-9215; www.yakitorirestaurant.com; Japanese; $$. Although this is a small restaurant—the seating only accommodates about 20 people—what it lacks in space, it makes up for in the quality of its food. Although sushi is prevalent on the menu, the standouts here are its namesake, yakitori (skewered grilled chicken), and *tonkatsu* ramen. The combination of pork and egg is exquisite. If you haven't eaten authentic ramen, get rid of any preconceived notions of it (i.e., forget the cheap, salty, packaged stuff you ate in college). Yakitori is *not* served at lunch, so make sure to visit at dinnertime to order it. The selection and portions of food are much better during the dinner hours. Closed for lunch on weekends.

Landmarks

Big Shanty Smokehouse, 3393 Cherokee St., Kennesaw, GA 30144; (770) 499-7444; www.bigshantybbq.com; Barbecue; $$. As far as barbecue restaurants, Big Shanty is one of the most notable in the Cobb County area. This restaurant staff is very friendly, and the place gives off a mom-and-pop vibe. For a sampling of the best the restaurant has to offer, be sure to get Steve's Sampler. This includes ribs, brisket, sausage, and pork. The platter also is available with 2 sides. The notable potato salad is quite delicious. The baked beans should not be missed, either. The beans spend time in the smoker, taking on that hickory smoked flavor themselves. Even if you aren't a traditional barbecue lover, the smoked salmon and turkey ribs (when available) are extremely tasty. Note: The restaurant closes at 5 p.m. on Sunday and is closed Monday.

C&S Oyster Bar, 3240 Cobb Pkwy., Atlanta, GA 30339; (770) 272-0999; www.candsoysterbar.com; Seafood; $$$$. Located in Vinings, C&S Oyster Bar is part of a strip mall; the valet parking is almost comical given that they share parking with a grocery store. However, once you get inside and sip on a cocktail, you'll forget you are in a strip mall and feel like you've been transported to a 1920s speakeasy. This restaurant is not for those on a budget, but more for a special occasion or those on an expense account. Enjoy a classic cocktail like a Pimm's Cup or a Sazerac or a new fancy cocktail like ginger limeade or the Westside. The wine selection is plentiful but most selections are by the bottle, so it's best to sample a few bottles with a group. Oysters are a must. C&S has an a la carte option and you can pick and choose which oysters you'd like to add to your order instead of ordering 6 of one kind and 6 of another. Oyster selection varies from New England to Washington, but all are extraordinary.

Although this is a seafood restaurant, steaks are on the menu and done well. Skip the pricey lobster tails and crab Legs in favor of fresh fish. Snapper, tuna, skate, sea bass, and flounder all are exceptional and available in a variety of preparations and sauces.

Canoe, 4199 Paces Ferry Rd. Northwest, Atlanta, GA 30339; (770) 432-2663; www.canoeatl.com; American; $$$$. This is a beautiful setting just on the cusp of Buckhead. Many choose Canoe to celebrate a special occasion, like an anniversary or birthday. The decor is lush and beautiful. Service is top-notch. The cuisine is upscale but not too fussy, meaning just about anyone can be satisfied by the dishes here. Start your meal with the shrimp-stuffed calamari. The calamari, crispy and not at all chewy, is complemented with slightly spicy Spanish chorizo. The Georges Bank cod is one of the most popular items and has been on the menu for years. For a more creative or inventive dish try the duck breast and duck sausage topped with cranberry-pistachio compote. Or try the Carolina rabbit with swiss chard, bacon ravioli, and sweet potato hash. However, one of the highlights here is their weekend brunch. The variety is outstanding, and the view of the outside patio, manicured lawn, and river just add even more to the ambience. Want a more casual, yet intimate evening? Book the private garden table outside (weather permitting). This picnic-style table allows for maximum seating overlooking the famous river. Dishes are served up family-style in a relaxed setting. Tip: Make sure you visit during daylight for the beautiful river view. Reservations recommended.

Marietta Diner, 306 Cobb Pkwy., Marietta, GA 30060; (770) 423-9390; www.mariettadiner.net; Diner; $$$. Just like its sister restaurant, **Marietta Fish Market** (see next page), the Marietta Diner remains one of the most popular restaurants in Marietta. The glowing neon signage illuminates the otherwise sleepy stretch of road during late hours. Upon entering the restaurant, patrons are immediately teased with the enormous display case of the decadent desserts that the diner has available. The diner serves breakfast, lunch, and dinner each day, and as such the menu (pages and pages long) has something for everyone. Patrons are treated to a complimentary spinach pie with each order. Although there are many Italian and Greek specialties on the menu, it abounds with options like pancakes, omelettes, wraps, sandwiches, burgers, fajitas, ribs, and pork chops. The portions are huge, and most diners walk away with take-out boxes, unable to finish a meal in one sitting. Service is always fast, friendly, and efficient. Even if you are too stuffed to order dessert, choose one and take it with you to go. The German chocolate cake and cheesecakes are quite extraordinary. Although the lot is large, it can be difficult to get parking on busier days. The diner is open 24 hours a day, 7 days a week, and even on holidays. In fact, it is full on Thanksgiving and Christmas.

Marietta Fish Market, 3185 Canton Rd., Marietta, GA 30066; (770) 218-3474; www.mariettafishmarket.net; Seafood; $$$. Everything about this Marietta favorite is large. The restaurant is huge and fills up early on weekends. Portions are pretty gigantic here as well. Food Network's Guy Fieri dined here shortly after they opened, creating instant fame for the restaurant. The nautical ambience extends from the lighthouse-themed entrance to the ship-decor theme inside the restaurant. Upon entering, diners walk by the display case of fresh seafood as well as very tempting desserts. Their rolls come with a highly addictive cream cheese spread, but save your sweet tooth for their delicious desserts. Appetizers are so large, they should be shared with at least 4 people. Skip the oysters in favor of the zucchini fries and grilled octopus. The fries are plentiful and pair quite well with the ranch dipping sauce. While the menu is filled with grilled, fried, and broiled seafood selections, to get a sampling try the platters, which come with shrimp, scallops, flounder, clam, catfish, and deviled crab. However, one of the most popular menu items remains the seafood paella—complete with a whole lobster tail, the size of this entree could easily feed a family of 4. Note that while the lunch menu is more limited, portions are still large and prices are much lower. On weekends the parking lot fills up early with families out for a meal. To avoid long waits, plan to arrive later (after 8 p.m.). Reservations are not accepted here.

Peter Chang's Tasty China II, 6450 Powers Ferry Rd., Sandy Springs, GA 30339; (678) 766-8765; www.petertasty2.com; Chinese; $$$. The name Peter Chang inspires much awe in Atlanta. The star chef opened up the wildly popular Tasty China in neighboring Marietta, and within a short amount of time the popularity of the restaurant had customers driving great distances to experience the authentic Szechuan cuisine. The restaurant itself is quite large and more upscale than his previous restaurant, Tasty China I. The menu itself is quite lengthy. To experience the most variety, the best approach is to visit with a large group and share dishes family-style. Some of the menu highlights are the dried fried eggplant, dan dan noodles, Shan City Chicken, fragrant duck, and the cumin lamb. Note that those used to more Americanized Chinese food might not care for the taste of this more-authentic cooking. These meals tend to be extremely spicy with hot peppers and on the salty side. A notable exception to this is the lotus roots and beef in a clay pot. Though it may sound unusual, the meal, served in large pot, is fragrant, and the beef, extremely tender. Although staff is very friendly, many don't speak fluent English and are a little green when it comes to making recommendations, especially for American palates.

Ray's on the River, 6700 Powers Ferry Rd., Sandy Springs, GA 30339; (770) 955-1187; www.raysrestaurants.com; American; $$$$. This beautiful restaurant overlooks the serene setting of Atlanta's Chattahoochee River. The outside is landscaped perfectly and, weather permitting, is worth walking around and even taking some pictures. The pristine setting is also a top choice for wedding rehearsal dinners, whether outdoors or in the nicely decorated interior with its dark woods and upscale decor. Not only is it an optimal choice for special events but for business dinners as well, as the menu offers seafood and prime cuts of steak. Start dinner with the barbecue shrimp and crab cakes (hands down some of the best in the city). Seafood is flown in daily, and the ginger-soy tuna and the Chilean sea bass are top choices. Steaks are perfectly done here as well. I recommend trying the rib eye, as it is extremely (almost fall-off-the-bone) tender. Prime rib lovers will enjoy the slow-roasted cut of meat, available in 12-, 16-, and 20-ounce servings. It is also one of the most in-demand brunch spots in the area, not only for the terrific views, but the classy brunch is phenomenal and offers lots of options to please everyone. Brunch options abound with nearly 80 selections including a carving station, peel-and-eat jumbo shrimp, a made-to-order omelette station, and an assortment of house-made desserts. Reservations recommended.

Roy's Cheesesteaks, 2900 Highlands Pkwy. Southeast, Smyrna, GA 30082; (404) 799-7939; Sandwiches; $. While Atlanta is not Philadelphia when it comes to cheesesteaks, the city does have a few places that do make a decent Philly cheesesteak. One such place is Roy's Cheesesteaks. While the sandwiches can be a little greasy, the taste is solid with a soft but substantial bun to hold in all the meaty goodness. I highly recommend adding the sweet peppers to the cheesesteak as it makes a huge difference in the taste. They also make a decent Italian hoagie. Service is lightning-fast on most days. The small sandwich is adequate for a filling lunch by itself with no other sides. However, a regular or large might be in order if you are famished. So if you are in a hurry to pick up a meal, this is good option. Little-known fact: This is one of the few places to serve birch beer, a carbonated soft drink made with birch bark and other herbal extracts. It is similar to root beer in taste. The drink washes down a cheesesteak pretty well, so it's definitely worth trying. Closed Sunday.

Scalini's, 2390 Cobb Pkwy. Southeast, Smyrna, GA 30080; (770) 952-7222; www.scalinis.com; Italian; $$. Located in a somewhat rundown strip mall, this Italian restaurant is a truly unexpected find. While the decor could use some updating—think '80s decor complete with plastic tablecloths—overlook this in favor of the extremely tasty Italian food. You'll start out with salad and garlic rolls served family-style. It will be tempting to fill up, but go easy, as there is much to try on the menu. Service is extremely friendly and helpful. Many of the staff have been working there for quite a while and can easily make recommendations based on taste preferences. Staff is happy to accommo-date special requests, and there are several vegetarian options as well as many classic chicken and veal options. The most popular menu item is the eggplant parmigiana. The layers of eggplant and ricotta are generously topped with a delicious and hearty meat sauce. There's even an urban legend that the dish induces labor. Many baby pictures adorn the wall of the restaurant, labeled "Eggplant Babies." The recipe is even available on their website. Tip: Get a free meal on your birthday; must show ID.

Trackside Grill, 2840 S. Main St. Northwest, Kennesaw, GA 30144; (770) 499-0874; www.tracksidegrill.com; Southern; $$. It doesn't get much more Southern than the Trackside Grill, located in downtown Kennesaw. The supersweet and friendly staff will make sure that your mason jar of sweet tea stays full. The corn muffins that accompany dinner have just the right amount of sweetness to them and won't ruin your appetite if you indulge in one or two. The menu is divided into lunch, dinner, and brunch, but it's supercute that each one has a section of "comfort plates." At lunch opt for the chicken salad sandwich or the fried green tomato sandwich. With its perfectly fried tomatoes, goat cheese mayo, and crispy bacon, it is truly a great representation of the South. Or to be very sinful, indulge in the macaroni and cheese. The huge portion comes with broccoli, mushrooms, and roasted red peppers in a 3-cheese sauce. Definitely add the andouille sausage. During dinner hours order the buttermilk fried chicken or the chicken potpie. Brunch is another good occasion to visit. Not only are there hits like the stuffed french toast and their signature Knife & Fork breakfast sandwich piled high with egg, bacon, gravy, and aged cheddar, but they also have the regular lunch menu available during this time as well. There are also tasty adult beverages like the citrus vodka cooler and the pomegranate margarita available as well. Restaurant is open for brunch only on Sunday.

Whistle Stop Cafe, 1200 Ernest W. Barrett Pwky. Northwest, Ste. 10, Kennesaw, GA 30144; (770) 794-0101; Southern; $. After a recent move into a larger space and more highly trafficked area, this Southern restaurant seems to be doing a tremendous business, especially at lunch. Its country decor, chalkboard menu, and, of course, train circling the restaurant all give it that Southern charm. By about noon each day, the restaurant it full, so don't be surprised to find a short wait for a table. The best items on the menu are fried items. (One exception is the collard greens, which regulars rave about.) Fried chicken is perfectly crispy with a light breading on the outside and tender and juicy on the inside. Sweet potato fries and fried green tomatoes are other hits. Chicken and dumplings and pork chops are solid choices, too. Lunches come with a choice of corn bread or biscuit. The biscuit is fluffy, soft, and much larger and tastier than the corn bread. There are also daily specials. The veggie platter comes with a choice of 4 vegetables. Waitresses have always been super friendly, and it is obvious that they have regulars who absolutely adore them.

Williamson Bros. BBQ, 1425 Roswell Rd., Marietta, GA 30062; (770) 971-3201; www.williamsonbros.com; Barbecue; $$. One of the long-standing barbecue joints in Cobb County, Williamson Bros.

has been serving barbecue for decades. At the time, there weren't many decent barbecue restaurants in the area, so the two brothers that started it brought all the skills they learned from their father to make true Southern barbecue. Their barbecue ribs, Boston butts, and pulled pork are cooked in a traditional wood burning pit. It may sound like a cliché, but the meat on the ribs is truly "fall off the bone." Their original sauce is slightly sweet and flavored with 16 spices. They've expanded to carry varieties like chipotle, honey BBQ and classic Carolina sauce among others. Although barbecue is delivered with some sauce on it, customers can add more with the various sauces that are on the table. Notable sides are the onion rings, Brunswick stew, and corn bread. For those not in the mood for pig, their catfish and burger are incredible. The restaurant has a tremendous seating area, including a decent-size outdoor area. The establishment does a fair amount of catering and is very dependable no matter the size of the crowd. Want to serve their sauce at home? They sell their special sauces and spices online.

Patak Meats, 4107 Ewing Road, Austell, GA 30106; (770) 941-7993; Butcher; $$. The line starts forming about an hour before the doors open, on the one Saturday each month that Patak is open. Steaks, pork chops, and sausages are all outstanding here. Sausages of all varieties can be found here—it's a true sausage fest. You can very easily walk out with two or three bags of high-quality meat for around $30. Say goodbye to prepackaged, filler- and nitrate-heavy meats. There is also a variety of Eastern European dry goods. Patrons drive long distances to shop here. The primarily Eastern European staff is friendly, helpful, and very efficient.

Sandy Springs, Roswell & Alpharetta

Sandy Springs has been noted as one of the most affluent zip codes in the country. Besides many multimillion-dollar homes in the area, there is much new construction with lots of brick and stone. Residents like their specialty markets and bakeries. This wealth has continued to spread north to the areas of Roswell and Alpharetta. Businesses have moved out into these areas as well. So expect to find high-end, pricier restaurants that cater to this crowd and fewer ethnic or cheap eats.

Amalfi, 292 S. Atlanta St., Roswell, GA 30075; (770) 645-9983; www.amalfiatlanta.com; Italian; $$. Start your meal off with an espresso martini. Eggplant parmesan and veal dishes are all excellent. Nightly specials are also top-notch. Service is warm and welcoming. Note that this isn't a place for young children. Tiramisu and ricotta cheesecake are worth saving room for. Reservations required on weekends.

Atlantic Seafood Company, 2345 Mansell Rd., Alpharetta, GA 30022; (770) 640-0488; www.atlanticseafoodco.com; Seafood; $$$$. This modern American restaurant serves seafood and sushi in an upscale atmosphere. It is not uncommon to find many business diners on weeknights. The usual suspects of shrimp cocktail, mussels, calamari, and crab cakes can be found on the starter menu. The chipotle mussels with cilantro and feta offer a departure from typical mussels. Fish is flown in daily. House specials include trout amandine, pecan-crusted mahimahi, and shrimp 'n' grits. Sushi is offered as well. Rolls like spicy tuna, rainbow, and dynamite are all to be found. They are decent, but true sushi aficionados may find it not authentic enough. They offer a decent variety of gluten-free menu items.

Bishoku, 5920 Roswell Rd., Ste. B-111, Sandy Springs, GA 30342; (404) 252-7998; http://bishokusushi.com; Japanese/Sushi; $$.

Although Bishoku is located in strip mall, the interior is very upscale and perfect for a romantic date night. The sushi bar is the focal point of the restaurant, with seating surrounding it in a U-shape. Some menu highlights are the fried squid legs and the glazed eggplant. For sushi try the fatty tuna or horse mackerel. At lunch opt for the bento box or pork shoga, a pork filet with ginger and soy. Of course the *tonkatsu* ramen is a good choice as well. There is a huge selection of sake. Organic sake has a floral taste, and there is even an apple-infused sake that is recommended at the end of dinner. Staff is extremely friendly, and most patrons are regulars who are fiercely loyal fans of the restaurant. Closed Sunday and Monday.

Brooklyn Cafe, 220 Sandy Springs Circle Northeast, Atlanta, GA 30328; (404) 843-8377; www.brooklyncafe.com; American; $$$. This casual neighborhood cafe boasts a fun and inviting patio. Open for both lunch and dinner, lunchtime includes mostly sandwiches, of which the pork tenderloin, Reuben, and vegetable are standouts. The vegetable with avocado, roasted red peppers, tomatoes, and Jack cheese is light and fresh. Whether visiting for lunch or dinner, don't miss out on their ever-popular California artichokes. Another good dinner starter is the Tomato Milanese, light enough to keep your dinner appetite. For entrees try the shrimp tacos, "Ever-Evolving" Salmon, or pork tenderloin.

Cafe Efendi, 37 Roswell St., Alpharetta, GA 30004; (770) 360-8014; www.cafeefendi.com; Mediterranean; $$. Whether at lunch or dinner, if you enjoy gyros, get the *doner* wraps, which are essentially the same thing but with a spicy tomato sauce. The buffet doesn't have a ton of offerings, so diners are better off ordering from the menu. Skip the more traditional hummus in favor of their very popular falafel as an appetizer. Don't miss the Turkish coffee. Late-night guests are treated to belly dancing. Hookah is offered here, too.

Cafe Sunflower, 5975 Roswell Rd. Northeast, Ste. 353, Atlanta, GA 30328; (404) 256-1675; www.cafesunflower .com; Vegetarian; $$. This vegetarian restaurant is extremely relaxing. There's an outdoor patio for warm spring days, although the interior is just as serene. When visiting with a group, get the Sunflower Box, which is a sampler of rolls, pot stickers, hummus, and spaghetti squash cake. The Jamaican black-bean cakes with pineapple salsa are wonderfully delicious, as is the garden lasagna. Spicy food lovers will appreciate the pad thai. Dessert is an absolute must at this restaurant. Try the chocolate torte or coconut cake. Closes early on Sunday.

Casa Nuova Italian, 5670 Highway 9 North, Alpharetta, GA 30004; (770) 475-9100; http://casanuovarestaurant.com; Italian; $$$. This cozy Italian restaurant serves authentic Italian dishes complete with home-grown organic vegetables. Who doesn't love garlic bread? But their hot Italian bread is extra addictive. This family-run restaurant aims to please customers, so it's not surprising to find owners greeting customers and checking in with them on their dinner. Customers rave about the chicken Francese, though there are many veal dishes as well. It is a popular spot for families hosting special events. Prices are very reasonable. Closed Sunday.

Cue Barbeque, 13700 Hwy. 9, #300, Alpharetta, GA 30004; (770) 667-0089; www.cuebarbecue.com; Barbecue; $$. This family-friendly barbecue restaurant churns out some very solid barbecue for the North Fulton folks. At lunch, opt for the barbecue chicken sandwich, with tender pulled chicken. Each customer has a favorite meat—ribs, brisket, pulled pork, sausage—they are all good choices. Ribs are huge and full of meat. Guests appreciate that the sides are of high quality, not an afterthought as they can be at some barbecue spots. The deviled egg potato salad is probably the best side, prepared with red potatoes and very little mayo. The fries are hand cut, and the mac 'n' cheese is prepared with high-quality cheeses. Save room for the bananas Foster dessert.

Firebird Rotisserie, 4719 Ashford Dunwoody Rd., Dunwoody, GA 30338; (770) 804-8288; www .firebirdatlanta.com; Pub; $$. This sports bar really wants to make sure that patrons don't miss a minute of the game—*any* game. All the booths are equipped with personal televisions in them. There's a good mix of patrons ranging in age—young professionals, people with small toddlers, and older folks. The fare is usual pub food: sandwiches, burgers, ribs, wings, and beer. However, as the name suggests, chicken is the highlight here, with the half rotisserie chicken being a feature. The pulled pork, buffalo chicken, and chicken Philly sandwiches and wings are all good bets. Ribs are an acceptable non-chicken option, too. Cocktails are exceptionally decent as well. Good for late-night food, as the kitchen stays open late. Tip: There's a late-night "deep-fried dessert" offering as-well. This includes fried Oreos, Snickers, Twinkies, and even hot dogs.

Genki Sushi, 5590 Roswell Rd., Ste. 100, Atlanta, GA 30342; (404) 843-8319; www.genki-inc.com; Sushi; $$. This popular sushi spot is located in the Prado shopping center, which is in the heart of Sandy Springs. Order a mango martini or Red Samurai from the bar. For starters don't miss the *hamachi kama* (yellowtail), which is crispy on the outside and tender and flaky on the inside, or any of the tuna appetizers. Seaweed salad is also worth trying. Note that there are a number of cooked entrees and noodle bowls at Genki as well, so it's a perfectly fine choice for non-sushi enthusiasts as well. Tip: Half-price bottles of wines on Wednesday night.

Hearth Pizza, 5992 Roswell Rd. Northeast, Sandy Springs, GA 30328; (404) 252-5378; www.hearthpizzatavern.com; Pizza; $$. This neighborhood gem cooks pizza in a 600-degree hearth oven, hence the name. The beer selection is worth mentioning, as there are 11 on draft and over 25 by the bottle. Start with the eggplant chips with a chipotle and sun-dried tomato aioli dipping sauce, or try their signature meatballs made with beef, veal, and sausage topped with ricotta. Choose from their signature pizzas or build your own. Highlights are the New Haven clam; ring of fire with chorizo salami, cremini mushrooms, and cilantro; and the shrimp and goat cheese with eggplant and olives. Tip: Mussels are half off on Monday, and pizzas are half price between 4 and 6 p.m. weekdays.

INC. Street Food, 948 Canton St., Roswell, GA 30075; (770) 998-3114; www.incstreetfood.com; Latin; $$. Located in the highly trafficked downtown Roswell area, INC. Street Food has embraced the street food movement with a twist. They've taken the food truck and moved it inside, sort of. The interior of the restaurant shows faux graffiti walls, and there's even a food truck replica that serves as a pass-through to the kitchen. The menu is a mixture of Latin specialties. The cactus and yuca fries are unique appetizers. Start out with one their refreshing waters like coconut or tamarind. *Bocaditos,* or appetizers, are large enough to substitute as full entrees. Try the calamari rellenos, stuffed with oxtail, or pork tamales. Tacos of barbecue octopus or veal cheek are quite adventurous too. Reservations not accepted.

Kozmo Gastropub, 11890 Douglas Rd., Alpharetta, GA 30005; (678) 526-6094; kozmogastropub.com; Gastropub; $$. Gastropubs in Atlanta are mostly located within the city; the outskirts seem to contain more family-friendly dining establishments with less adventurous menus, so Kozmo is a breath of fresh air in the Alpharetta neighborhood. Located at the end of a strip mall, you could almost miss it if you aren't on the lookout. Stepping inside, the open kitchen and minimalist decor are reminiscent of sleek Midtown restaurants. Specialty cocktails are creative, especially the gin gin. Start with the panko-fried eggplant drizzled with honey. Comfort food like mac 'n' cheese, brisket, and fish-and-chips are the menu. However, the *poutine*—french fries topped with cheese, gravy, and brisket—is a menu highlight. Opt for pasta dishes when offered, as the soft and tasty pasta is house-made.

Lucky's Burgers and Brew, 1144 Alpharetta St., Roswell, GA 30075; (770) 518-5695; www.luckysburgerandbrew.com; Burgers; $. This canine-friendly establishment is a rather new Roswell joint, opened in 2010. Although sandwiches and salads are offered, this remains a burger-centric restaurant. Start your meal off with fried pickles or the tempura artichoke hearts. Choose from their custom burgers or build your own. Turkey, bean, or chicken can be substituted for beef. The Lucky Burger, served with side and drink, is only $7. Creative burgers include the Poodle Chaser with brie, caramelized onions, and Dijon. They have old-school beers (Carling Black Label, Genesee Cream Ale, etc.) offered in cans for a relatively low price. They allow dogs on their patio, so feel free to bring your pooch when the weather allows.

Madras Chettinaad, 4305 State Bridge Rd., Alpharetta, GA 30022; (678) 393-3131; www.madraschettinaad.com; Indian; $$. You won't find a more beautifully appointed Indian restaurant in the city. Stepping inside and seeing the high-end furnishings in this spacious and immaculately decorated spot, it is easy to forget it is located in a strip mall. During weekdays, nearby office workers pack the restaurant at lunchtime to take full advantage of the numerous buffet offerings. While there are plenty of vegetarian curries and dishes on the buffet, there are still a number of meat-centric entrees as well. The chicken tikka masala and chicken 65 are both highlights. At dinner, order off the vast menu. Start with samosas. *Thalis* are a good option for those wishing to try a variety of small dishes, and biryani rice dishes are tasty. However, curry dishes (lamb, chicken, or shrimp) as well as the butter chicken are some of the best. Wash your meal down with a sweet mango lassi or refreshing coconut water. They also have a large room for private parties.

Mambo Cafe, 11770 Haynes Bridge Rd., Ste. 601, Alpharetta, GA 30009; www.mambos-cafe.com; Cuban; $$. Go easy on the *aji* sauce that you are served to dip the bread, as it is tasty but very hot. Regulars love the *ropa vieja,* tender shredded beef sautéed with peppers and onions. Pork and seafood dishes are menu highlights. Try the *chuletas de puerco al adobo,* or pork chops marinated in garlic and onions. Paella is tasty but does take 30 minutes to prepare. Call ahead to save yourself time if you want to have this Latin classic. The restaurant tends to be a favorite of office workers nearby for lunch, so it does fill up during lunch hours. Visit at dinner for a less-crowded space.

Milton's Cuisine and Cocktails, 780 Mayfield Rd., Alpharetta, GA 30009; (770) 817-0161; www.miltonscuisine.com; Southern; $$$. Milton's Cuisine is housed in a historic building—a converted farmhouse actually. The decor complements the farmhouse character with antique mirrors on walls and other elements to keep the old-fashioned charm of the building. They have a vegetable garden, which produces most of the vegetable and herbs used in their foods. The seafood comes primarily from the Gulf of Mexico and is extremely fresh. Start with the distinctly Southern fried green tomatoes or the sweet potato and shrimp fritters. Entree highlights are the shrimp and grits and the sesame-crusted trout. The chef likes to come around to tables and make sure dinner is satisfactory. Wine list has many options.

Mirage Persian, 6631 Roswell Rd., Ste. C, Atlanta, GA 30328; (404) 843-8300; www.miragepersiancuisine.com; Persian; $$. This Persian restaurant serves up a decent lunch on weekdays. Instead of traditional hummus, start the meal off with one of the two house-special eggplant appetizers. While there is no shortage of kebab dishes of chicken or beef, the *joujeh* kebab offers something unique: a Cornish hen with a saffron-citrus marinade. Vegetarians will enjoy the *shirin polo* or wedding rice, steamed basmati rice with almonds, pistachios, currants, and orange zest in a saffron-rosewater sauce. Reservations required for weekends. Don't forget to save room for baklava dessert. Note: Lunch specials are very reasonably priced.

Never Enough Thyme, 5354 McGinnis Ferry Rd., Alpharetta, GA 30005; (678) 297-1124; www.neverenoughthyme.net; Sandwiches; $. This breakfast and lunch spot also doubles as a caterer. In addition to breakfast options of omelettes and quiches, their lunches are hot and cold sandwiches, salads, and pastas. The chicken salad and the Jersey Joe sandwiches are some of the most popular menu items. There is also a section of prepared foods for those who need to grab dinner on the way home from work. Think chicken Marsala, lasagna, meat loaf or pot roast—all comfort foods. The clientele is mostly nearby office workers or housewives having a leisurely lunch after a tennis match.

Ray's Killer Creek, 1700 Mansell Rd., Alpharetta, GA 30009; (770) 649-0064; www.raysrestaurants.com; Steaks; $$$$. *Top Chef* contestant Tracey Bloom is really killing it with a revamped menu at this upscale establishment. Always a popular destination for business dinners, it has recently added some more eclectic and lower-price options. Huge and pricey steaks, like the gigantic rib eye, are still available, but Chef Bloom has brought other more affordable offerings to the menu, like a flatbread of the day—a sample one is topped with prosciutto, roasted red peppers, arugula, and truffle oil. The veal Bolognese and short ribs are other options that are high on taste, but a little lighter on the wallet. Reservations required.

Rice Thai, 1104 Canton St., Roswell, GA 30075; (770) 640-0788; www.goforthai.com; Thai; $$$. This little Thai restaurant is located just off the Roswell Square. During peak hours it gets cramped, as the restaurant is a renovated house. Visit during nonpeak hours for more space. Spring and fall days make a porch seat an absolute must. Start with the coconut soup with chicken or shrimp. While noodle dishes are just fine, it is the curry dishes that keep customers coming back. The red curry in particular is a customer favorite. Not in the mood for a sit-down meal? They do a large take-out business, so call in your order.

Rumi's Kitchen, 6152 Roswell Rd., Atlanta, GA 30328; (404) 477-2100; www.rumiskitchen.com; Persian; $$$. The decor is pretty upscale, which sets this Persian restaurant apart from some of its counterparts in the area. Upon being seated, the table is treated to a complimentary plate of bread with walnuts, olives, feta, radishes, and mint. Start the meal off with *kashk badenjoon* and hummus. Kebabs of shrimp or chicken are quite tasty and have tangy kick to them. Rack of lamb or lamb shank are customer favorites. Note: There are no vegetarian options here. Reservations required.

Satay House, 281 S. Main St., Alpharetta, GA 30004; (770) 663-8666; www.satayhouseatlanta.com; Thai; $$. Though there is much Thai food on the menu, there's also some Chinese dishes to be found on the menu at Satay House. The namesake, satay chicken, is a customer favorite, but those who like hot and spicy foods won't be disappointed by the Satay House either. The spicy coconut soup is killer, and they do a delicious red curry and Massaman curry. The roti cani, which is basically round bread served with some curry for dunking, is a treat as well. Don't forget to order a Thai iced tea to wash your meal down. (Tip: Lunch is a fantastic deal. For under $10, you'll get soup, salad, and a decent-size entree. Dinner portions are very generous, too.)

Sushi Nami Japanese, 5316 Windward Pkwy., Alpharetta, GA 30004; (678) 566-3889; Sushi; $$$. Located in the northern suburb of Alpharetta, this is a favorite sushi spot for those who live and work nearby. Sit at the bar and watch the chef work his craft, preparing the sushi before your eyes. Although the sushi is slightly pricier than that found at other nearby establishments, the quality is much better. One of the more unusual rolls is the strip steak roll, prepared with slices of raw steak topped with crab. There's also a fairly decent section of cooked foods as well, for dining companions who don't do sushi. Hibachi served with soup and salad to start is also a good value.

Swallow at the Hollow, 1072 Green St., Roswell, GA 30075; (678) 352-1975; www.theswallowatthehollow.com; Barbecue; $$. Menu items here are prepared using organic and locally grown ingredients if possible. The ribs or chopped pork are solid, and the sauce is quite tasty. Pork is tender and juicy. Vegetarian options include a smoked portobello mushroom and fried green tomatoes. Regulars rave about the mac 'n' cheese. Banana pudding is interesting in that it has chocolate chips instead of vanilla wafers. The porch and entire outdoor seating area are lovely. Visitors love to enjoy leisurely meals on warm days. Tip: They have live music on weekends. Reservations aren't accepted, so expect long wait times on weekends.

Teela Taqueria, 227 Sandy Spring Place, Ste. 506, Sandy Springs, GA 30328; (404) 459-0477; www.teelataqueria.com; Mexican; $$. Fun is the best way to describe Teela Taqueria. Located in the City Walk shopping center, this lively and bright taqueria is just the kind of restaurant that the shopping center needed. Specialty drinks here are mojitos and margaritas. Start off with the trio of salsa, guacamole, and cheese dip. The salsa is especially fresh-tasting, like something made in-house rather than poured out of a jar. Bang bang shrimp (shrimp with a chile aioli) and the shrimp and crab (crab and shrimp cake with chipotle cream cheese) tacos are a must for seafood lovers. The Southern BLT taco is interesting as well— bacon, lettuce, and fried green tomatoes (that's where the Southern part comes in) with feta cheese and smoky chile aioli. But the chorizo taco is divine; the marriage of spicy chorizo with salty feta and sweet dates is a perfect combination. For dessert, you can't go wrong with tres leches or flan.

Tin Can Fish House and Oyster Bar, 227 Sandy Spring Place, Ste. 502, Sandy Springs, GA 30328; (404) 497-9997; www.tin

canfishhouse.com; Seafood; $$. Located just next door to **Teela Taqueria** (see previous page), this rustic-looking seafood establishment has the same owners. Diners can even order off either restaurant's menu. The decor evokes memories of past visits to beachy waterfront cafes. If the decor doesn't make you feel like you just stepped off the boardwalk, the food sure will. Starters of bang bang shrimp, mussels in cilantro-coconut curry, or the ahi tuna are all hits. The menu has po'boys, for those so inclined, but for only a few dollars more, get the fish, prepared to your liking with 2 sides. While preparation can be blackened, sweet chile–glazed, horseradish crusted, and the always popular fried, the most popular seems to be blackened grouper or mahimahi.

Veranda Greek Taverna, 11235 Alpharetta Hwy., Ste. 105, Roswell, GA 30076; (678) 330-1218; www.verandagreektaverna .com; Greek; $$$. Opa! There's a lovely patio for alfresco dining. Staff is attentive and knowledgeable. Start with the octopus or mussels in ouzo. Also, don't miss the halloumi cheese, which is brought to your table in a flaming skillet. Try the traditional moussaka—eggplant and ground beef topped with béchamel—or the lamb-stuffed phyllo. Many of the menu items are gluten-free. There's live music on weekends, and most weekdays offer half-price hookahs. Tip: Visit on Sunday, as they offer tapas on special for $5 each.

World Peace Cafe, 220 Hammond Dr., Ste. 302, Sandy Springs, GA 30328; (404) 256-2100; www.worldpeacecafeatlanta.com; Vegetarian; $. This vegetarian spot located in Sandy Springs is unique in that it is run completely by volunteers and donations. That's right, the servers are volunteers. Decorated with large paper lanterns, it has loft-like feel to it. Orders are placed at the counter and brought to diners shortly after that. There are several decent options of omelettes and frittatas for breakfast. The peace burger is the signature dish and a customer favorite. Try some of the varieties including the Jamaican burger, Texicali, or Southern cheeseburger with pimiento cheese. The potato wedges served as a side are baked, not fried, but still packed with flavor. There's a lunch special for around $5 of half a sandwich and soup. For soups think tomato basil, or lentil, kale, and mushroom, which most customers rave about. They also offer organic teas and coffees, which are all 100 percent fair-traded.

Wright's Gourmet Sandwich, 5482 Chamblee Dunwoody Rd., Dunwoody, GA 30338; (770) 396-7060; www.wrightgourmetshoppe .com; Sandwiches; $. This is definitely a more upscale sandwich place, but in no way snooty. Staff is very friendly. The menu is listed on two huge blackboards that you can't miss when you enter the restaurant. Try the New Orleans classic, muffuletta, oozing with cheese and very hearty. The Rebel Reuben, made with turkey, is also a customer favorite. Skip the side of chips in favor of their house-made sides like potato or broccoli salad. Desserts like the red velvet cupcake or lemonade cake are irresistible. The restaurant also caters, offering many cakes and pies as well as boxed lunches. Closed Sunday.

Xian China Bistro, 5316 Windward Pkwy., Alpharetta, GA 30004; (770) 442-9996; http://xian-chinabistro.com; Chinese; $$$. Named for a city in China where the ancient Silk Road started, Xian China Bistro has an extremely friendly staff, making regulars feel like family. The decor is pretty upscale with a beautiful mural of the 3rd century BC terra-cotta warriors, clay replicas of China's first emperor, Qin Shi Huang's, army. There are approximately 8,000 of these clay soldiers, who were sculpted to protect the emperor in his afterlife and discovered in 1974. The restaurant is dimly lit, but fancy lighting illuminates the bar and individual tables, and patrons can hear the peaceful sounds of an in-house waterfall. Even when the spacious restaurant gets busy, the noise level isn't too loud. You could quite easily have a business lunch or date night and hear each other just fine. Customer favorites are the pine nut chicken and, for those who enjoy spicy foods, the spicy orange-peel lamb.

Landmarks

Aqua Blue, 1564 Holcomb Bridge Rd., Roswell, GA 30076; (770) 643-8886; Seafood; $$$$. Its sleek, modern interior could fool you into thinking you were in an upscale Buckhead or Midtown restaurant. As you walk inside, there is a curtained-off room to the right of the hostess stand for private parties. Behind the hostess stand is a large bar area with plenty of high-top tables and, because it is so beautiful, you could enjoy your entire meal there. The main dining area is pretty snazzy itself, with white booths and nicely appointed light fixtures, and of course the cozy patio beckons on warm evenings. Skip cocktails and dive right into the wine list. Servers can help with wine recommendations. Start with the sweet-and-spicy calamari, tempura green beans, and jumbo lump crab cake. Ask for the half-and-half options of calamari and green beans, as the portions are huge. The sea bass is quite delicious, with the slightly crunchy exterior giving way to the buttery insides. Tip: Sign up for their e-mail list and get a free lobster any day during your birth month.

Bistro VG, 70 W. Crossville Rd., Roswell, GA 30075; (770) 993-1156; www.bistrovg.com; French; $$$$. The mostly white decor, walls, and tables give the overall feel of a modern minimalist look, but the off-white French fabrics on chairs lend a little warmth to the overall feel. The chic decor and somewhat adventurous menu make it a unique find in the Roswell suburb. Start with the white bean truffle soup, crab cake, or mussels. Small plates of gnocchi and grilled octopus are a steal at $10 or less. Fish and seafood entrees, with the exception of the short ribs with spicy mac 'n' cheese, outshine meat entrees. There's a prix-fixe menu for $29 for those who are price-conscious, though that menu is quite limited.

Cabernet, 5575 Windward Pkwy., Alpharetta, GA 30004; (770) 777-5955; www.cabernetsteakhouse.com; Steaks; $$$$. Cabernet was one of the first destination restaurants in the Alpharetta area and was a pleasant shift from the local chain restaurants. Service is very attentive. Many businesses located in the neighborhood have meetings here. At lunch, the prime rib sandwich is a hit. Start with the lobster bisque with its huge chunks of seafood. Any steak is well worth having here. The price is on par with many of the top steak houses in the country, and so is the quality. There is an enclosed cigar bar attached to the restaurant, and some diners appreciate an after-dinner smoke.

Canton Cooks, 5984 Roswell Rd. Northeast, Atlanta, GA 30328; (404) 250-0515; Chinese; $$. Located in a strip mall that shares space with Whole Foods, you'll meander to the back of the shopping center to get here. Weekends can be crowded, but waits are not long. Although this is a Cantonese restaurant, it specializes in Americanized Chinese dishes rather than more authentic Chinese cuisine. That being said, those dishes are rather tasty. Try the salt-and-pepper squid or the spare ribs, with a sweet sauce that is almost candylike. Fish maw and crab-meat soup as well as the snow pea leaves are customer favorites. Standard dishes like General Tso's chicken and Mongolian beef are popular dishes here. Open late night until 2 a.m. each day.

Dinner & a Movie

Greater Atlanta offers some unique movie and dining experiences. What's better than a one-stop date night?

Fernbank—Martinis and Imax Theatre
Fernbank Museum adds some fun to nightlife with their martinis and Imax (767 Clifton Rd., Atlanta, GA 30307; 404-929-6300; American; $$), which has been running with much popularity for approximately 15 years. The museum shows short nature films (about 40 minutes) on its large Imax screen. Bartenders serve up swanky cocktails, and a pretty diverse menu is available. Starters include perennial favorites like hummus, quesadillas, nachos, and spinach dip. While entrees like fish, lasagna, and steaks are available, the menu features sandwiches and pizzas, too. So there is something to please everyone. Advance purchase of tickets is a must, as most shows sell out. Note: shows offered on Friday night, except in November or December, when the museum is rented out for special events.

Starlight Drive-In
Starlight Drive-In (2000 Moreland Ave. Southeast, Atlanta, GA 30316; 404-627-5786; www.starlightdrivein.com; Snacks; $) has been delighting patrons for decades. The thrill of a drive-in theater still appeals to many, even in the age of the high-tech multiplex theaters with the ultimate in surround sound and stadium seating. Starlight is as much about tailgating with friends as it is about the movie. Many like to bring a small table and chairs and set up a couple hours before

the movie starts. This affords you the best spot and view. There is a snack bar with typical movie snacks such as popcorn and candy, but most prefer to bring their own food. Keep in mind that you'll need a battery-powered radio, folding chairs, food, drinks (alcoholic beverages are allowed), and a blanket for cool nights. They show 2 movies per screen and the cost is only $7 per person and only $1 for children age 9 or under.

Studio Movie Grill

Located in the north suburb of Roswell, **Studio Movie Grill** (2880 Holcomb Bridge Rd., Alpharetta, GA 30022; 770-992-8411; www .studiomoviegrill.com; American; $$) is relatively new. Everything about this dine-in movie theatre is pretty state of the art. You can reserve tickets and even seats in advance, so there isn't a rush to arrive much before the show's start time. The modern-looking lobby even has a bar where you can enjoy a cocktail before or after your movie. Might I suggest a jumbo margarita? There's plush seating in theaters and servers have handheld devices for order entry. Wings and salads are available as normal starters, but the jewel is the Megaplex Burger. Complete with onions, mushrooms, and different cheeses, it is a filling and delicious meal to enjoy while watching the latest flick.

Five Seasons Brewing, 5600 Roswell Rd., Atlanta, GA 30342; (404) 255-5911; http://5seasonsbrewing.com; American; $$$. Five Seasons is a unique restaurant, not only specializing in its own unique brews, but also an organic menu. Beer aficionados will appreciate the offerings, which change regularly. The menu is much better than what can be found at a standard pub. Start with the grilled shrimp and grit cake or the alligator eggrolls. Their pizzas, offered on a thin crust, are quite tasty as well (think Granny Smith apples and serrano ham), and menu highlights are the duck breast and rabbit enchiladas. There's even a large patio for group functions or get-togethers. Reservations suggested for weekends.

Goldfish, 4400 Ashford Dunwoody Rd., Atlanta, GA 30346; (770) 671-0100; www.h2sr.com/goldfish/; Seafood; $$$. Located in close proximity to Perimeter Mall, it is a terrific place to visit after a day of shopping. But don't mistake it for a typical chain restaurant. This classy seafood restaurant is luxurious (it has a 600-gallon saltwater aquarium), and the food quality is high-end and fresh. No matter how you like your fish, they will prepare it to your liking. Highlights are the barbecue salmon, trout, and the Hong Kong sea bass. They also have a solid offering of sushi rolls. Servers are helpful at making recommendations, especially if you're unsure about wine. On busy nights it can get quite noisy in the dining room, so it's perhaps not ideal for a romantic evening. Note that there are several gluten-free options here. Tip: Choose 3 small plates for $15 any day of the week.

Horseradish Grill, 4320 Powers Ferry Rd. Northwest, Atlanta, GA 30342; (404) 255-7277; www.horseradishgrill.com; Southern; $$$$. This restaurant has been popular with Atlanta residents for many years; however, Rachael Ray made it extremely popular when it was featured on *$40 a Day*. Located rather close to the open-air Chastain Park Amphitheatre, it is a popular choice before concerts there. Start with the tempura-fried okra. Their signature dish is their fried chicken; many visiting from out of town are big fans of it. Steaks, grouper, or Georgia trout are all solid choices. While the interior of the restaurant is classy and well-appointed, the patio is secluded, with trees and plants surrounding it, and it's well worth spending an evening there. They are quite popular for brunch, too.

Indigo, 1170 Canton St., Roswell, GA 30075; (678) 277-9551; www.indigoroswell.com; American; $$$$. Popular with the locals for special occasions, Indigo is high on quality and romance. The interior is intimate and cozy, but the outdoor patio is where you'll want to be on warm evenings. Start with the crispy shrimp with pineapple salsa or the house-made charcuterie plate. Don't overlook the creative salads; try the strawberry salad with spiced pecans in honey-lime vinaigrette or prosciutto and panzanella salad with pecorino and basil dressing. Entrees offer a diverse sampling of items like the chicken-fried duck, lamb porterhouse, or cumin scallops. Inventive sides like Key lime coleslaw or blue cheese hash browns are delightful as well.

Joey D's, 1015 Crown Pointe Pkwy, Atlanta, GA 30338; (770) 512-7063; www.centraarchy.com/joeyDs.php; Steaks; $$$$. Named for the famous Oak Room restaurant in New Orleans, Joey D's serves up quality steaks and blends Cajun flair with many menu items. Don't be fooled by the nondescript brick exterior, because the inside of the restaurant is well-appointed and classy. Joey D's clientele seems to be a mix of business diners, couples, and friends in their late 30s and early 40s. Their house-made croissants with drizzled honey are superb. Fans love the she-crab soup and oyster shooters. Steaks are the signature dishes here. Try the garlic strip steak. The bar is bright and lively with table-to-ceiling displays of liquor, perfect for dining at if there is a long wait for a table.

Nori Nori, 6690 Roswell Rd., Sandy Springs, GA 30328; (404) 257-1288; www.norinori.com; Japanese; $$. Most sushi lovers may not be fans of a buffet, but this buffet is quite fresh, and staff brings out new offerings quickly. Besides sushi there are many other foods offered here: salads, oysters, crab legs, chicken dishes, and desserts. Dinner buffet offers a wider selection of goods. Lunch buffet is nearly half the price. Make sure to explore all areas of the buffet

With a Laugh

The **Punchline** comedy club (280 Hilderbrand Dr., Atlanta, GA 30328; 404-252-5233; www.punchline.com; American; $$), around for decades, has seen some very famous acts in its time. There are small tables for couples or double dates and large tables perfect for group outings. Although seating can be pretty tight, they always have acts that will keep you laughing. From the well-known (think Craig Shoemaker, Louis CK, Dave Chappelle) to the unknown, all their comics are extremely entertaining. Although the menu is standard pub fare, the chicken cheesesteak is a standout. They state a two-drink minimum policy.

area, because it is large, and you'll want to be aware of all the goods that are available.

Platinum Blue, 4505 Ashford Dunwoody Rd., Dunwoody, GA 30346; (770) 551-9900; http://platinumbluesushi.com; Sushi; $$$. This small sushi restaurant is located in the Park Place shopping center across from Perimeter Mall in the heart of Dunwoody. While the restaurant does open during dinner hours, it really doesn't get crowded until after 9 p.m. But it can get rather loud and clubby then, so for a quieter evening arrive earlier rather than later. The atmosphere is pretty sexy with blue lights. Outdoor dining can be cramped, so opt for indoor seating when possible. Servers are friendly and helpful in making recommendations. Be careful not to fill up on the complimentary shrimp chips. Tuna tartare is fresh and tasty. The Platinum Blue Roll is a house special.

Sage Woodfire Tavern, 11405 Haynes Bridge Rd., Alpharetta, GA 30004; (770) 569-9199; www.sagewoodfiretavern.com; American; $$$$. Sage is terrific for a girls' night out or a date night. Try the seared sea scallops with creamy mascarpone risotto, tomato confit, and sautéed seasonal vegetables with vintage port reduction. Steaks are all top quality as well. There are also daily specials that are quite sublime too. Think Chilean sea bass with lobster risotto. Can't decide between meat or seafood? They offer several surf and turf combos as well. Tip: Lounge and bar are open late night until 2 a.m., and there are half-price bottles of wine on Sunday.

Salt Factory, 952 Canton St., Roswell, GA 30075; (770) 998-4850; http://saltfactorypub.com; Pub; $$$. Don't be fooled by the name, Salt Factory serves up some extremely tasty entrees in this rustic and historic building. The wood floor and exposed brick walls lend a rich yet cozy feel to this high-end pub. Located in the heart of Roswell, some patrons enjoy stopping for a pint, but it is the food that brought the Food Network here to profile the restaurant. The cheeses and charcuterie plate are quite unusual and should not be missed. They even come with house-made dipping sauces. The shepherd's pie, however, is the dish that made the restaurant world famous. It is made with lamb instead of beef and is spiked with cumin. Served in a cast-iron skillet, it is definitely a pretty large portion of comfort food. Surprisingly, the wine list seems more robust than the beer list, even though it is a pub.

Specialty Stores & Markets

Alpine Bakery, 12315 Crabapple Rd., Ste. 100, Alpharetta, GA 30004; (770) 410-9883; www.alpinebakeryandtrattoria.com; Bakery; $$. In an odd combination, this bakery, started in 1996, sells both desserts and pizzas. The stromboli, a huge piece of dough filled with cheese, pepperoni, and sausage, is a customer favorite. Note that there are many vegetarian options as well. The house-made gnocchi is not to be missed. This bakery is an impressive place with cookies, cakes, tarts, and all sorts of dessert items.

Breadwinners, 220 Sandy Springs Circle, Atlanta, GA 30328; (404) 843-0224; www.breadwinnercafe.com; Bakery; $. As the name suggests, the restaurant sells bread. But these loaves are more of a dessert than those used for a sandwich. The variety is tremendous and these breads have funky names like the Papa Don't Peach or the Party at My Place Pumpkin. Popular flavors are the cranberry and pumpkin. Although the loaves are pricey at $15, they are quite tasty. Many choose to get the 3-pack variety, which comes in a gift box wrapped with a bow, to give as gifts around the holidays. They also have a cafe that serves soups, salads, and sandwiches like the caprese or tuna melt with tomatoes and Muenster cheese, both menu highlights. Closed Sunday.

E. 48th Street Market, 2462 Jett Ferry Rd., Dunwoody, GA 30338; (770) 392-1499; www.e48stmarket.com; Italian/Markets; $. This family-run market, located in the Dunwoody, is part Italian deli, part high-end grocery store, and part bakery. There are Italian pastas, sauces, and cheeses and other imported specialties to be found. Sausages and mozzarella cheese are prepared in-house. The prosciutto-and-mozzarella sandwich and meatball sandwiches are menu highlights. If dining in, browse the dessert section and don't leave without trying a cannoli. Staff is extremely friendly. They also can help make recommendations from their growing wine selection.

Jolie Kobe Bakery, 5600 Roswell Rd., Atlanta, GA 30342; (404) 843-3257; www.jolikobe.com; Bakery; $$. What's unique about this bakery is that it is Japanese-French fusion. There's a terrific offering of breads (try the curry bread), pastries, and chocolates. Sandwiches at lunch are quite tasty, too. Try the egg salad or shrimp or crab cake. Tip: They are open for brunch on weekends. Instead of waiting in long lines at other nearby restaurants, head here and dine on pancakes and delicious crepes without waiting.

Pie Hole Desserts, 1025 Canton St., Roswell, GA 30075; (678) 461-3776; http://openyourpiehole.com; Bakery; $. As one might guess, this establishment makes pies that are piled high with quality and delicious ingredients. Try the apple crumb, chocolate derby, chocolate peanut butter, and blackberry pies. Strawberry pineapple and Almond Joy are unique pies, too. Want a pie that isn't dessert? They also make chicken potpie. They also offer high-quality teas.

Sally's Bakery, 5920 Roswell Rd., Ste. 108a, Sandy Springs, GA 30328; (404) 847-0211; www.sallysbakery.com; Bakery; $. This no-frills bakery is located just off Roswell Road near I-285. What makes Sally's Bakery unique is that they cater to those with gluten intolerance. They make gluten-free buns (for burgers or sandwiches). There are lots of other breads and dessert items as well. The chocolate chip cookies are the highlight here. Even though they are gluten-free, they are still high on flavor. Note that this establishment is pick-up only. There is no place to sit. Closed Sunday.

Atlanta's Food Trucks & Stands

According to Edward L. Glaeser, a professor of economics at Harvard University and director of the Rappaport Institute for Greater Boston (in a quote from the *Boston Globe*), "food trucks are a natural part of the innovative culinary process. . . . Preserving the monopoly power of local eateries is a terrible reason to restrict food trucks." There is a big push to bring more food trucks to the Atlanta area. The process has been slow, but we are making progress. There are several food trucks that are successfully operating in the Atlanta area.

Delia's Chicken Sausage, 489 Moreland Ave., Atlanta, GA 30316; (404) 474-9651; www.thesausagestand.com. Delia's Chicken Sausage is the latest entry into the food truck/stand arena, offering a unique menu featuring locally produced chicken sausage. The sausage is organic and hormone-free, and Delia has a recipe that she's been keeping a secret for 15 years. The most popular menu is the Slinger, a delicious handcrafted chicken sausage. If you'd like a little kick in your chicken, give the Hot Mess slinger with chili, cheese sauce, and jalapeños a try. The Three Way slinger, topped with coleslaw, chili, and sauerkraut, is another crowd pleaser. Adventurous foodies should get the Double D Delight slider, made with a Krispy Kreme doughnut and chicken sausage patty. For vegetarians, all slingers can be made without meat.

Good Food Truck (http://goodfoodtruckatl.com). Food served in a waffle cone sounds weird, right? But true to the idea of street food, they've created a food that is easy to carry while you walk down the street. Flavors are influenced by many cultures, including Indian, Asian, and Mexican. Sample items include crispy rice dessert with almonds, figs, and paprika. The Poodle, a hot dog served in a french-toast hot dug bun, topped with apple maple slaw, spicy mustard, and maple syrup is a customer favorite.

Incredible Flying Soup Mobile If you've heard of **Souper Jenny** (see p. 16), the Buckhead cafe with tasty soups and sandwiches, then you can only imagine how delicious the goods from this food truck are, as it is owned by Souper Jenny. Besides the delectable soups and sandwiches available, the Incredible Flying Soup Mobile is known for its lobster rolls.

King of Pops (www.thekingofpops.net). Truly a unique and innovative concept, the King of Pops was started by Steven Carse. He was a laid-off office worker who decided he didn't want to go back to the daily grind. Starting out very small, he started making fresh fruit ice pops, which he sold out of his cart located in the Midtown/Va-Hi area of North Highland and North Avenue. He updates followers as to changes of location or daily menus via social media sites Twitter and Facebook. Popular flavors include blackberry mojito, grapefruit mint, banana cinnamon, and chocolate sea salt, among others.

Streatery (240 Peachtree St. Northwest, Atlanta, GA 30303; www.streatery.com). These are some of the best dogs in the city. You can get all-beef or pork sausage. Toppings are amazing. You could go with something simple like chili, mustard, sauerkraut, and the regular onions. You could even order barbecue sauce and guacamole on your dog if you like. Vegetarian? They've got you covered. Streatery offers a soy dog, too.

Tamale Queen (www.queenfoodco.com). This food truck serves authentic Mexican tacos and tamales based on homemade recipes. Food is prepared fresh and served on the spot. Offerings are tacos—steak, chicken, pork, fish, and veggie—as well as their signature tamales and a delectable flan for dessert.

Tex's Tacos (www.texstacos.com). Dubbed the Antonio Banderas of food trucks, Tex's Tacos serves up tasty tacos and quesadillas.

Their *al pastor* (pork) taco is probably the most unusual—served with a topping of sweet pineapple. Tip: They are one of the few food trucks that accept credit cards. Try the side of lime fries, a little bit salty and a little bit sweet.

Yumbii (www.yumbii.com). What do you get when you combine Mexican and Korean foods? Some of the most delicious creations available, also known as Yumbii. The Yumbii food truck serves tacos, burritos, and quesadillas with your choice of beef, chicken, pulled pork, or tofu. Tacos and burritos are topped with Korean barbecue sauce and sesame seeds. Don't miss the sesame fries topped with chile peppers and served with a side of chipotle ketchup. If you want to try a more expanded menu, visit **Hankook Taqueria** (see p. 92) in Midtown.

Local Chains, Wineries & Breweries

Every city has local chain restaurants—places with multiple locations within the city limits. These are restaurants that locals love no matter what their food preference is. These restaurants are pleasing to all Atlantans. They've been around for quite a while and have garnered a loyal following.

Cafe Intermezzo, www.cafeintermezzo.com; Desserts; $. Although Cafe Intermezzo has a food menu, it is the desserts and coffees that have been dazzling patrons for years. Although the interior is a beautiful space in and of itself, with cozy tables and candlelight, the patio remains the most popular spot to snag a table. With its wrought iron and trees popping up through the floors, it is a beautiful space to gather with friends or end a dinner date. The coffee and drink menu is thicker than the food menu. Full of exotic coffees, teas, and drinks, there is certainly something for everyone on the menu. If a nutty taste is what you like with a hint of sweetness, opt for the Suisse Mokka or the Spanish Mokka. For non-coffee drinkers, give the Mexican chocolate a try, a dessert by itself for sure. True coffee connoisseurs will appreciate the Turkish coffee, which comes in its own carafe. The desserts do not have a menu, as they change daily. Once seated, make your way to the dessert display case and choose from their many cheesecakes and pies. The attendant will write your selection down and give it to you, which you hand to your server once back at your table. A little unorthodox, but all part of their kitsch. All desserts are fabulous, and you can't go wrong with anything.

El Taco Veloz, www.tacoveloz.com; Mexican; $. With a handful of Atlanta locations, this authentic taco joint is barely a chain. The smallish tacos pack a lot of flavor in them. Two soft corn taco shells envelop the meat and other goodies and keep the filling inside. When making a meal of them, 2 or 3 will fill you up. The *al pastor* (pork) is one of the best on the menu, although the *barbacoa* (brisket) is quite tasty as well. This isn't the kind of place that gives you chips and salsa with your meal. The staff doesn't speak much English, but it is relatively easy to decipher the menu. The restaurant is a haven for those in Cobb County desiring authentic Mexican because there aren't other authentic options in the area, and the tacos here are extremely tasty and inexpensive (all under $2). They also have tasty *tortas,* burritos, and tamales. Don't miss out on having a *horchata* with your meal. This is a sweet drink made with rice milk. If you are in a super hurry, they also have a drive-through.

Fellini's Pizza, www.fellinisatlanta.com/fellinis.html; Pizza; $. All locations of this late-night pizza favorite are located inside the Perimeter. While all 7 locations are open until midnight, several are open until 2 a.m. Visitors come here not only for the fantastic pizza, but also the fun atmosphere. Many Fellini's pizza shops are located in former garages that have been refurbished, although some of the original elements, like the doors, have been retained to keep a unique look in the space. They are painted in bright colors and have a fun vibe. Many also feature a large outdoor patio that patrons fill on warm days and evenings. As for the pizza, it can be ordered by the pie or by the slice. By the slice is far more popular. Choose from regular thin-slice or thick Sicilian. Pepperoni and sausage are certainly winners, as is the spinach and mushroom. Slices are huge, and one slice should satisfy a normal appetite. Salads here are also very large and come with quality ingredients, including lots of fresh mozzarella and black olives. Groups love to order pitchers of beer and enjoy their pizza at leisure.

Flying Biscuit, www.flyingbuiscuit.com; Southern; $. **Open** for breakfast, lunch, and dinner, so stop in anytime but don't miss out on the biscuits. These are flaky and just about melt in your mouth. Breakfast is served all day. Breakfast options abound with platters, scrambles like the Southern Scramble with spicy collard greens, and specialty omelettes like the Clifton with goat cheese, mushroom, and basil. While the Flying Biscuit is known for breakfast foods, dinner options are quite tasty as well. Stop in for the shrimp 'n' grits. The shrimp are decent-size and plentiful, blending well with the creamy grits. Another good choice for dinner is the salmon with Coca-Cola glaze. Note: There are many vegetarian options on the menu.

Highland Bakery, www.henrisbakery.com; Bakery; $$. With locations in Buckhead, Midtown, and the Old Fourth Ward, the latter remains the most popular. The bakery has fresh-baked bread along with other dessert items. On weekends locals pack this place to the brim in their quest for a delicious brunch. Expect to wait, as reservations are not taken. Among the menu highlights are the sweet potato pancakes, cilantro corn pancakes, and peanut butter french toast. For a more meat-centric dish, order the cowboy Benedict or the fried chicken Benedict, two fried chicken patties on top of a biscuit with a poached eggs and jalapeño cheese sauce. Come hungry, as portions are enormous. They also serve sandwiches, soups, and salads.

La Fonda Latina, www.fellinisatlanta.com/lafonda.html; Latin; $. Sister restaurant to **Fellini's Pizza** (see p. 216), located next door. This is a destination for inexpensive Latin food. The food is delivered quickly in a fun atmosphere (opt for outdoor seating whenever possible). The ingredients are always fresh and high quality. Don't miss out on the beef enchiladas, spinach and shrimp quesadillas, vegetarian paella, or *arroz con pollo* (chicken and rice).

Papi's, www.papisgrill.com; Cuban/Latin; $. Papi's Cuban and Caribbean restaurant brings Latin flavors to you. Start with the *hallaca,* Chile's version of the tamale. Menu highlights are the *ropa vieja* sandwich with tender sliced beef, onions, and peppers, or *masitas de puerco,* an authentic Cuban dish with cubed pork marinated in Cuban spices and *mojo* sauce. Each day has a daily special, which is reasonably priced. Sandwiches are large and hearty and easily make a good dinner meal as well as lunch. Order the *media noche*—a Cuban sandwich on sweet bread. Skip regular fries in favor of yuca fries as they are more flavorful.

Roasters, www.roastersfresh.com; Southern; $. Roasters' menu consists of mainly chicken dishes, but sides are distinctly Southern: mac and cheese, fried okra, corn bread. The rotisserie chicken and wings are exceptionally tasty here. The skin on the outside is crisp, but the inside is moist and bursting with flavor.

Super H Mart, Asian/Specialty market. This is an Asian specialty foods and grocery store. They carry all sorts of rice, noodles, snacks, dried foods, and even ready-to-serve foods. They even stock health and beauty items and appliances. Currently there are five Super H Marts in the Atlanta area, all located in the northwest metro area, which has the highest concentration of Asians.

Breweries

Red Brick Brewing, 2323 Defoor Hills Rd. Northwest, Atlanta, GA 30318; (404) 881-0300; www.redbrickbrewing.com. Red Brick Brewing is a little smaller than **Sweetwater Brewery** (below), but the cost is the same: $8. This buys a souvenir glass and 4 tastes. Tours are Wednesday through Friday from 5 p.m. until 8 p.m. One highlight is that they allow patrons to bring in food from nearby establishments. So feel free to pick something up on the way and enjoy it while sipping on some of their beer. During warm months, the crew even sets up fun games outside like table tennis and corn hole. Tip: They have a terrific event space, perfect for reunions or company parties.

Sweetwater Brewery, 195 Ottley Dr. Northeast, Atlanta, GA 30324; (404) 691-2537; www.sweetwaterbrew.com. Sweetwater Brewery tours are every Wednesday, Thursday, and Friday evening and Saturday from 2:30 to 4:30 p.m. During weekdays, the doors to

Sweetwater Brewery open at 5:30, and they have about 3 tours per evening, every half hour beginning at 6 p.m. They like to have everyone out by 8 p.m. at the latest. Also, plan on eating before or after, as there are no munchies offered. Parking fills up quickly but is available throughout the various lots near the brewery. The neighboring businesses are closed by then and allow patrons to park in the lots for free. But by about 6:30 p.m. almost all parking is full, so if you don't want to walk too far, arrive early. The tour is free, but to sample beer, you'll need to buy tickets. For $8 you get a souvenir glass with 6 drink tickets. Pours are half a glass, maybe three-quarters of a glass from the more-generous employees. If they give you a good pour, it is a nice gesture to tip them well.

Wineries

Montaluce Winery, 501 Hightower Church Rd., Dahlonega, GA 30533; (706) 867-4060; www.montaluce.com; $$$. About 1.5 hours north of Atlanta, in Dahlonega, Georgia, is a beautiful winery called Montaluce. The entire design is reminiscent of a small Italian village. Montaluce Vineyards is not only a winery, but on-site they also have homes for sale, and there are plans to build a resort and special events facility. Right now, they host a lot of weddings, as the scenery is quite breathtaking. The restaurant on-site, **Le Vigne,** boasts stunning views overlooking the vineyards.

Bill, the resident sommelier, escorts guests through the various rooms used in their winemaking and thoroughly describes the winemaking process. He demonstrates the different equipment used in making red versus white wine and explains how the two processes differ. Montaluce hosts free wine tours on Saturday at 2 p.m., according to Bill.

Le Vigne at Montaluce overlooks the vineyards and has an upscale decor. Enter the main lobby with its high ceilings, and to the left is a counter where wine tastings take place. Stay for dinner on the patio or in the well-appointed dining room. Most nights there is a 3-course meal that consists of locally sourced items. Try the roasted cauliflower soup, tender pork loin, or Georgia trout.

Persimmon Creek Vineyards, 81 Vineyard Ln., Clayton, GA 30525; (706) 212-7380; www.persimmoncreekwine.com. Persimmon Creek is another wonderful getaway from the city, located in Clayton, Georgia. The 22-acre winery was named a Top Ten Hot Small Brand in 2011 by *Wine Business Monthly*. Unusual wine offerings include Cabernet Franc, Seyval Blanc, and even Icewine. Persimmon Creek wines are served at many upscale Atlanta restaurants including the Ritz-Carlton. An interesting fact about the land that is now Persimmon Creek is that it was once the site of moonshine stills. Fact: The winery is powered by solar energy.

Recipes

Here are some recipes from some of my favorite Atlanta restaurants. Some are old favorites with a new spin on them, like the Macaroni and Cheese. Others are new recipes that I've tasted and just fallen in love with.

Babette's Cafe Steamed Mussels with Strawberries & Serrano Peppers

Serves 2

Strawberry Serrano Base

1 cup strawberries, washed and
    hulled
1 serrano pepper, deseeded
¼ teaspoon minced garlic
¼ teaspoon minced shallots
½ teaspoon Coco Lopez or
    coconut milk

Process all ingredients through a food processor until completely smooth.

Mussels

2 pounds mussels, washed and
    cleaned
Strawberry Serrano
    Base (above)
¼ cup heavy cream
2 tablespoons unsalted butter
2 tablespoons white wine
Juice from ½ lemon
Salt and pepper to taste
Chive sticks for garnish

Combine all the ingredients, except chives, in a skillet. Toss well.

*Cover with a lid and cook on medium high heat
until mussels are open, about 5–6 minutes. Pour
into a bowl and top with chive sticks.*

Recipe courtesy of Babette's Cafe (p. 62).

Livingston Braised Short Ribs

Serves 4–6

Brine

2 quarts water

½ cup salt

½ onion, cut into ½-inch dice

1 small carrot, peeled and cut into ½-inch segments

1 celery rib, cut into ½-inch segments

1 tablespoon pickling spice

4–6 pounds crosscut beef short ribs (bone-in)

Combine all ingredients, except short ribs, in a large sauce pot and bring to a boil.

Reduce heat and simmer 10 minutes to dissolve the salt.

Chill completely.

Once the brine is completely chilled, pour over the short ribs and let them soak in the brine for a minimum of 24 hours.

Braising

Oil for browning short ribs

All-purpose flour for dusting short ribs

4 cloves garlic, crushed

½ large onion

1 carrot, split lengthwise

2 ribs celery, cut into 4-inch segments

2 tablespoons tomato paste

2–4 quarts chicken stock (low sodium if using packaged)

Large sprig of fresh thyme

Salt and pepper to taste

Preheat oven to 325 degrees.

Coat the bottom of a Dutch oven with ⅛-inch of oil and place over medium high heat.

Drain the short ribs from the brine. Roll the short ribs in flour and pat off any excess.

Once the oil is hot, sear the short ribs until they are deep brown but not burnt. Remove the short ribs from the pan and place on paper towels to rest.

Pour off all but a small amount of the oil, reduce the heat to low, and add the garlic, onion, carrot, and celery. Sauté for 3 minutes. Add the tomato paste and stir. Let the tomato paste caramelize slightly.

Add the short ribs back to the pot, cover with stock (it is very important that the meat is completely submerged), and add the thyme. Bring to a gentle boil on the stove top and then transfer the covered pot to the oven

Braise for 4 hours; ribs should be very tender.

Scoop the ribs out of the liquid and set aside. Strain the braising liquid to remove the vegetables.

Simmer the braising liquid on the stove top to reduce by approximately half its volume to enrich the flavor. Season with salt and a pinch of black pepper to taste.

Add the short ribs back into the sauce to coat. Enjoy.

Recipe courtesy of Livingston (p. 93).

Parish Mushrooms & Grits

Stone Ground Grits

Serves 6

8 cups water
3 tablespoons butter
Salt and pepper

2 cups stone-ground grits, such as Logan Turnpike or Nora Mill

Combine the water and butter. Bring to a boil. Whisk in the grits. Reduce heat to a slow simmer. Simmer, whisking frequently, until the grits are tender and creamy, about 25–30 minutes. Season to taste with salt and pepper.

Roasted Mushrooms

3 pounds wild mushrooms, such as oyster, hen of the woods, or trumpets, cleaned

4 tablespoons olive oil
Salt
Pepper

Preheat oven to 375 degrees. Toss the mushrooms in the oil. Season to taste with salt and pepper. Roast until tender, about 12–15 minutes.

Pecan Gremolata

Zest of 3 lemons
Zest of 2 oranges
3 tablespoons finely chopped parsley

⅓ cup chopped pecans
1 cup extra-virgin olive oil
Salt and pepper

Mix all ingredients together. Season to taste with salt and pepper.

To serve, spoon the grits into a large platter or casserole dish. Top with roasted mushrooms and drizzle with gremolata.

Recipe courtesy of Chef Joe Schafer of Parish (p. 69).

10 Degrees South Bobotie

Serves 4–6

- 1½ cups onion, chopped
- 2 cloves garlic
- 2 pounds ground beef
- 2 tablespoons olive oil
- Salt and pepper
- 2 to 3 tablespoons curry powder (depends on how spicy you want it to be)
- 1 tablespoon ground turmeric
- 1 cup brown sugar
- 1 cup apricot preserves
- 2 Granny Smith apples, peeled and grated
- 1 cup raisins
- 2 bay leaves

Sauté onions and garlic in oil until soft and translucent. Add ground beef, salt, and pepper and stir until the meat has browned. Add curry powder, turmeric, brown sugar, and apricot preserves. Stir until well combined, then add the grated apple. Let it cook for about 5 minutes, then add the raisins. Once the raisins have plumped up (after about 5 minutes), take the mixture off the stove and drain any excess oil (and there will be some—it depends on how much fat content is in the ground beef you buy).

Let the mixture cool down, then put a couple of bay leaves in the bottom of your dish, and then add the mixture.

Custard Topping

- 3 eggs
- 1 cup milk and a little cream (optional)
- Salt and pepper
- Cinnamon

Preheat oven to 375 degrees. Beat all custard ingredients together and pour over the meat. Bake for about 30 minutes until golden brown.

Recipe courtesy of 10 Degrees South (p. 30).

Two Urban Licks Crab Beignets

Yield: 10

6 cups flour

2 cups corn flour

2 tablespoons baking powder

3 tablespoons kosher salt

1 tablespoon cornstarch

4 cups 2 percent milk

1 egg

1 cup crabmeat

½ cup fresh corn kernels

½ cup grated manchego cheese

Mix all dry ingredients in a mixing bowl until well blended. Add the milk and egg. Fold the mixture together until well saturated. Once completed, fold in the crab, fresh corn, and manchego cheese.

Take the completed mixture and form into loose balls approximately the size of a meatball. Place them into a deep fryer set at 350 degrees for 3 minutes. Remove from the fryer. Place on paper towels to soak up the excess oil.

Place on a plate and garnish with the jalapeño glaze (below).

Jalapeño Glaze

3 jalapeño peppers

1 cup sugar

2 cups water

½ sheet gelatin

Salt and pepper to taste

Cut open and deseed the jalapeños, removing the tops as well. Place the jalapeños and sugar into the water. Bring to a boil. Boil the jalapeños until extremely tender. Blend the mixture together in a food processor until jalapeños are pureed.

Add the gelatin to the mixture and let cool. Season with salt and pepper.

Recipe courtesy of Two Urban Licks (p. 78).

Wisteria Macaroni and Cheese

Yield: 8 12-oz. servings

7 tablespoons unsalted butter, divided, plus additional for the baking dish

1 teaspoon kosher salt

2 cups dried elbow macaroni

1 pound collard, mustard, or turnip greens

¾ teaspoon finely chopped garlic

2 tablespoons all-purpose flour

2 cups heavy cream

2 teaspoons finely chopped fresh parsley

2 teaspoons finely chopped fresh thyme

1 teaspoon finely chopped fresh sage

½ teaspoon finely chopped fresh rosemary

⅛ teaspoon cayenne pepper

½ teaspoon salt

¼ teaspoon freshly ground pepper

½ pound grated New York sharp cheddar cheese

⅓ cup panko (Japanese bread crumbs)

Heat oven to 350 degrees. Butter a 2½-quart, deep casserole dish and set aside.

Fill a large pot with water. Bring to a boil, and add 1 teaspoon salt and the macaroni, reduce heat to a low boil and cook al dente (until it offers a slight resistance when bitten into), about 9 minutes. Empty the macaroni into a colander to drain.

Rinse and remove tough stems from the greens. Pat dry and cut into strips. Heat the Dutch oven over medium-high heat. Add 2 tablespoons butter and garlic and heat until butter is melted and garlic is fragrant, about 1 minute. Add greens and gently stir until wilted, about 4 minutes. Add cooked greens to the macaroni in the colander and drain. In the same Dutch oven, heat 4 tablespoons butter with flour over medium heat and stir for 3 minutes. Gradually add the cream and stir until thickened.

Mix the parsley, thyme, sage, and rosemary in a small bowl. Stir the cayenne, salt, and pepper and half the herb mixture into the cream sauce. Mix the collards and macaroni into the cream sauce in the Dutch oven.

Spread a layer of greens and macaroni in the casserole, layer with cheese, repeating the layers with remaining ingredients until casserole is full. Top with the panko and remaining herbs. Dot the top with remaining butter. Bake until bubbly and golden brown, about 45 minutes.

Recipe courtesy of Wisteria Chef Jason Hill (p. 79).

LEARN TO COOK

The **Cook's Warehouse** (www.cookswarehouse.com) is the spot to hit up if you are a foodie who loves to cook or a novice just getting into it. They have all sorts of cooking classes to suit any level. Classes are taught by nationally known chefs like Virginia Willis, Gena Berry, and Rebecca Lang, as well as some of the top local chefs from Atlanta restaurants. After you watch the cooking demo, you'll get to eat what the chef and you cooked during the class.

In addition to offering cooking classes, the Cook's Warehouse is a store that features all kinds of cooking accoutrements and gadgets. From the simple garlic peeler to the Swiss Diamond Crepe Pan to the popular Big Green Egg grill, you'll find whatever cooking essentials you need to get started or cook your meal for a large dinner party. The staff is also very friendly and helpful in getting you exactly what you need. There are four Atlanta locations: Decatur, Midtown, East Cobb, and Brookhaven.

The staff at **Viking** (1745 Peachtree St. Northeast, Atlanta, GA 30309; 404-745-9064; www.vikingcookingschool.com) is extremely knowledgeable and more than happy to help point you in the right direction or answer any questions. The Viking store is definitely made for foodies who have money to spend on high-end cookware and gadgets. Classes are relatively small, around 10 people. Instructors teach basic knife skills and tips like how to cut an onion without crying and how to tell when fried chicken is done. They offer classes for children starting at age 7.

Appendix: Eateries by Cuisine

Ecco (Midtown), 89
Iberian Pig (Gwinnett/Decatur), 118
Olive Bistro (Cobb & Northwest
   Atlanta), 158
Portofino (Buckhead), 14
Simpatico (Cobb & Northwest
   Atlanta), 162
Social (Downtown), 48
Truva (Downtown), 49

Mexican
Bone Garden Cantina (Midtown), 85
El Myr (Downtown), 35
El Norteno (Buford Highway), 134
El Pastor (Buford Highway), 134
El Taco Veloz, 215
Holy Taco (downtown), 40
No Mas (Downtown), 43
Original El Taco (Virginia Highland/
   Inman Park), 69
Raging Burrito (Gwinnett/
   Decatur), 122
Sausalito West Coast (Midtown), 96
Taqueria del Sol (Midtown), 97
Taqueria El Rey Del Taco (Buford
   Highway), 139
Teela Taqueria (Sandy Springs, Roswell
   & Alpharetta), 194
Zapata (Gwinnett/Decatur), 125

Persian
Mirage Persian (Sandy Springs,
   Roswell & Alpharetta), 190
Rumi's Kitchen (Sandy Springs,
   Roswell & Alpharetta), 192

Pizza
Antico Pizza (Midtown), 100
Athens Pizza (Gwinnett/Decatur), 125
Big Pie in the Sky Pizzeria (Cobb &
   Northwest Atlanta), 148
Fellini's Pizza, 216
Fritti (Virginia Highland/Inman
   Park), 66
Harry's Pizza and Subs (Cobb &
   Northwest Atlanta), 152
Hearth Pizza (Sandy Springs, Roswell
   & Alpharetta), 186
Mulberry Street Pizza (Cobb/ NW
   Atlanta), 157
Peace, Love and Pizza (Cobb &
   Northwest Atlanta), 159
Quattro (Midtown), 95
Rosa's Pizza (Downtown), 46
Varasano's Pizza (Buckhead), 31

Pub
Brick Store Pub (Gwinnett/Decatur), 126
Cypress Street Pint & Plate
   (Midtown), 88

Index